Hands-On

PHYSICAL SCIENCE

Hands-On
PHYSICAL SCIENCE

75 Real-Life Activities for Kids

Laurie E. Westphal

 PRUFROCK PRESS INC.
WACO, TEXAS

Library of Congress Cataloging-in-Publication Data

Westphal, Laurie E., 1967-
  Hands-on physical science : 75 real-life activities for kids / Laurie Westphal.
     p. cm.
  ISBN-13: 978-1-59363-237-3 (pbk.)
  ISBN-10: 1-59363-237-1
  1. Physical sciences—Study and teaching (Middle school)—Activity programs. 2. Physical sciences—Study and teaching (Elementary)—Activity programs. I. Title.
  Q181.W475 2008
  372.35--dc22
                        2007037836

Copyright ©2008 Prufrock Press Inc.

Edited by Lacy Elwood
Production Design by Marjorie Parker

ISBN-13: 978-1-59363-237-3
ISBN-10: 1-59363-237-1

At the time of this book's publication, all facts and figures cited are the most current available; all telephone numbers, addresses, and Web site URLs are accurate and active; all publications, organizations, Web sites, and other resources exist as described in this book; and all have been verified. The authors and Prufrock Press make no warranty or guarantee concerning the information and materials given out by organizations or content found at Web sites, and we are not responsible for any changes that occur after this book's publication. If you find an error or believe that a resource listed here is not as described, please contact Prufrock Press.

Prufrock Press Inc.
P.O. Box 8813
Waco, TX 76714-8813
Phone: (800) 998-2208
Fax: (800) 240-0333
http://www.prufrock.com

Contents

Chapter 1

Introduction

According to Webster's Dictionary, physical science is defined as "any of the natural sciences (as physics, chemistry, and astronomy) that deal primarily with nonliving materials." Everything we do and encounter on a daily basis is somehow impacted by the physical sciences, from the simple act of walking to speaking with others.

Interdisciplinary Impacts of Physics

Physics does not exist in a world unto itself. In fact, it is what makes the world in which all other processes exist and function. In terms of curriculum subjects, physics crosses into most other disciplines.

- *Mathematics*—Mathematics is a cornerstone for most physical science concepts. In order to record physics data accurately, students need to choose appropriate units and accurately read measurement tools. Once measurements are recorded, mathematics plays an important role in various calculations and manipulations of data in order to draw appropriate conclusions.
- *Language Arts*—Language arts and physics are deeply connected. When conducting experiments, it is critical that the data obtained and the conclusions drawn can be communicated in a clear and concise manner through expository writing. The other connection occurs when students are asked to process physical science concepts in a new and creative way through creative writing.
- *History*—Physical science discoveries have had significant impact on history. Developments by scientists have impacted the quality of life throughout history. By investigating the inventions and discoveries during each historical time period, these scientific discoveries often are the missing piece that explains why certain progress was made that could not have been done previously.
- *Research Skills*—Science is research based in nature. Although often skipped because of time constraints, the second step of the scientific method is to research the problem, finding out what others have already discovered about the proposed scientific problem. In order to find this information, students must become good researchers.
- *Oral Communication Skills*—After experiencing an activity, students often are asked to communicate their thoughts and ideas with their classmates. The more often they

discuss their ideas using appropriate scientific vocabulary, the more proficient they become not only in science, but also in speaking and defending their ideas. Students also spend time creating presentations that are shared with classmates, who will in turn provide constructive criticism for the betterment of future presentations.

<table>
<tr><td>

Why Is This Book Needed?

</td><td>

It seems that either teachers really enjoy this content, or they really dread it. Those who enjoy it love to see the looks of surprise and wonder on their students' faces when the students encounter unexpected results, or see an everyday concept in a new way for the first time. Those who dread the physical side of science usually have the fear of what could go wrong with the "whiz-bang" demonstrations or experiments, or if the students ask a higher level question about the concept.

</td></tr>
</table>

Everyone knows that there are great hands-on experiences for students in the physical science areas. Although they definitely command the attention of the students, sometimes students can get caught up in the excitement and miss the point of the experience. The focus of this book is to share a balance between the exciting and the important concepts taught in physical science. This book strives to meet this need for balance.

Most physical science concepts are abstract in nature. We can view the results or examples of physical science concepts, but you cannot bring Newton's first law of motion for show and tell, as you could a vertebrate. The idea that this branch of science is abstract often makes it more difficult for students to understand. Therefore, this book helps make the abstract more concrete, yet it also maintains the validity of the concepts.

This book introduces and reinforces key physical science concepts appropriate for grades 4–8. Activities and products were specifically chosen to meet the National Science Education Standards (NSES). When looking at the standards for teaching science, NSES examines the shift in the way in which the instructional process should be implemented. This shift is quite clear. The focus of the standards calls for the change in instruction from *teacher centered* to *student centered*. The standards suggest that all students are not alike and the interests, experiences, and needs of the individual students should be taken into account during the learning process. This should include how the teacher designs and chooses activities, lessons, and products for his or her students. The standards also focus on the idea that scientific inquiry should have a primary role in the presenting and processing of information rather than simply the use of lectures and texts. The standards also call for a movement away from recitation of acquired knowledge, instead providing opportunities for students to discuss and debate the scientific concepts being presented. It is clear that the students and their needs should be the primary focus in science education.

The lessons and activities included in this book were chosen for their appropriateness in meeting the National Science Education Standards. The activities ask students to discuss, process, and experience scientific knowledge. The products that drive the instruction encourage student choice, are open-ended, and reinforce key scientific processes. The various labs that were selected encourage individual scientific thinking rather than simply answering questions—whether they take the students through the scientific process on their own as in experimental designs or expose students to a unique experience, asking them to process the information gained in their own way. The 75 various labs, activities, and products contained in this book encourage the students to become independent scientific thinkers.

Chapter 2

Using This Book

The physical science concepts in this book are divided into both larger units that are product based and smaller units that are more exploratory and experiential in nature, without a significant product. The units are presented in the order that I used when teaching these concepts in the classroom, but many districts' scope and sequences will vary. Each unit certainly can be taught in whatever order best meets the curricular needs.

Unit Formats   Each large unit is product based. The first lesson of the unit will introduce the product, its rubric, samples, and the expectations for each criterion to guarantee an excellent product. The second and sometimes third lessons are introductory and more concrete in nature. They usually will directly tie into the product so students see an immediate use for the concepts being taught. If the product requires a culmination presentation, or sharing, this will always be the last lesson in the unit. The other lessons in each unit usually are activities or experiments that ask students to apply and extend the unit concepts at a higher level. Although I have included them in the order in which I taught them, the lessons can be used in any order. They also can be used to supplement other lessons being used in the classroom.

Each smaller unit is more exploratory and inquiry based in nature. It does not include a product. These units were selected to be shorter because they rarely are taught or assessed separately from other content. For example, some teachers will combine the concepts of states of matter or fluid laws with chemistry units, while others choose to teach them with heat and energy. These lessons are intended to be integrated easily into other larger units as the curriculum dictates.

Products   Each larger unit is centered around a significant product that the students will work on completing as the unit progresses. It is intended that the product and its rubric will be introduced during the first few days of the unit. In order for students to create quality products, they need to understand the expectations for each criterion. Based on the questions and clarifications I have made throughout the years when using these rubrics, I have included detailed explanations for each criterion when appropriate, to create a better picture of the possibilities for each product, as well as explanations about why some of these seemingly strict guidelines are important. Sometimes a product criterion will include an opportunity for "extra credit." In theory, I am not a big believer in extra credit, especially in the form of worksheets, crossword puzzles, or word searches. The only time students could earn extra credit in my class was by going above and beyond in the creation of their product. Therefore, there will be references to extra credit opportunities in some of the rubrics.

One of the aspects of several rubrics is the $1 rule. This requires that the student does not spend more than $1 on his or her product. Teachers can alleviate student woes about finding materials by providing some materials or keeping a "junk box" with materials for students to use in their products. Some of the product rubrics ask that students create a theme or decorate their products. These themes should allow the teacher to recognize the student's product based on knowledge of his or her interests.

Once the product is introduced, all of the activities that follow will supplement important aspects of the product. By using the product-based unit, students automatically have a tie-in for the information being presented. How often do students ask, "When will we ever use this?" By initiating the product and building excitement and interest before any activities take place, students will know immediately that they will use the concepts being taught.

All of the products included are highly interesting and challenging. They have been chosen because they represent different learning styles and varied interests of the students. Each year, my students were asked to evaluate labs, activities, and products and choose their favorites. The products included in this book consistently were chosen as favorite products throughout my years in the physical science classroom.

Lab Philosophy

When choosing lab experiences and activities, there are different philosophies that can be considered. The biggest debate concerns how much information should be given to the students in a lab situation. This book tries *not* to provide standard "cookbook" experiences. Instead, whenever possible, students are asked to think about their ideas, make their own predictions, and if possible, record their own procedures that they will then test. Although this may seem like it is not enough guidance for the students (and teachers) it actually is very appropriate. For example, by allowing students to develop their own predictions, students may observe or question something that was not originally intended by the lab but is an excellent hypothesis that could be investigated. If the lab had been completely structured from start to finish, the student would not have varied from the "cookbook" to think of other ideas not originally intended. Therefore, to encourage this open questioning and thinking, certain lab experiences will seem exceptionally open-ended (see experimental design section on the following page.) The more we can encourage our students to think about and question what they see, the better scientific thinkers they will become.

Whole-Group Labs/Activities

Most units (depending on the number of activities and materials) have at least one whole group lab experience. Every teacher has his or her preferred structure and procedure for lab reports, whether students record all the information for their labs in a composition book (the method I used), on a blank generic lab report used for all labs, or on a paper lab report for that specific lab. I also know some teachers who choose to mix it up depending on the lab and the amount of writing involved. I have tried to write the labs in this book in such a way that they could be used with any of these teacher-preferred methods. If it takes longer to write the procedure and create the data table than conduct the experiment, providing the information on a lab sheet may be a better option. Taking into account the procedures and data tables, the amount of time to conduct the experiment and the complexity of the directions, I sometimes provided a student lab sheet that follows the teacher pages in order to facilitate the experience. If a student lab sheet was not necessary, but there were processing questions, these would be included after the teachers' pages, as well. When conducting experiments in the classroom, in order to conserve paper, I would either post the questions or make group copies for student reference when creating their lab report. In general, all of the labs follow the scientific process from the purpose or problem, to collecting data, processing questions, and stating their conclusions.

I have included one lesson (Lesson 1) at the end of this chapter that I always used at the beginning of the school year. It allows the teacher to introduce observations (qualitative/quantitative) and inferences, as well as reinforce your preferred lab report format. It also sets the tone for the year about questioning the obvious, which is the basis for physical science concepts.

Rotational Labs

Some of the units have rotational labs as a key experimental component. These rotational labs are card based; all of the instructions are intended to be duplicated onto card stock and then laminated for durability. Rotational lab experiences usually are shorter and more exploratory in nature. Teachers have the flexibility to choose which mini-labs they would like to use, although usually it is best if at least two to three more mini-labs than groups are set up in the classroom. That way, groups can easily differentiate themselves as they move freely to any open station, taking a little more time at those that they need to think about more deeply than others.

Rotational labs solve the problem of limited supplies and managing equipment. Rather than the teacher needing multiple sets of equipment (one for each group in their classroom), by using rotational labs, they only need one set. This also allows the teacher to set up some "high-maintenance experiences" that they may not otherwise feel comfortable doing with the entire class, but really would like everyone to experience. These experiences may include using an open flame, hotplates, or projectiles. By using a rotational lab structure, the teacher can control the number of these types of experiences, and be in close proximity to those groups.

These rotational labs can be set up two different ways: as "bucket labs" or "rotation stations." To set up bucket labs, buckets will be assembled in which all of the materials and instructional cards for a particular lab are placed in tubs in a central area of the room. Groups can then take a tub back to their station to complete their experience. After completing the experience, they can exchange their tub for another one. This also allows for more than one of each bucket to be set up depending on equipment availability. Rotation stations also can be set up at fixed stations that the students rotate through in an orderly or random fashion depending on space in the classroom. When I was in the classroom, if possible, I would try and reserve a larger space so the students could spread out and move at their own pace. If the larger space was not available, and I had six groups, I would try and use at least 8–10 rotational options so that when students rotated in order, there was usually an open station in front of them. This way, they could still rotate at their own pace.

Experimental Design Labs

Many of the units include an experimental design experience. These labs are a little different than a typical lab because the instructions given to the students may seem quite sparse. A successful experimental design lab poses a question and provides a list of predetermined materials and certain required guidelines to solve the problem or answer the posed question. Given this information, students experiment with various variables and designs to find the most successful ones that solve the problem. Students actually are most successful when the teacher does not have preconceived notions about the best way to solve the problem. This way, it is easier for the teacher to keep students focused on their individual ideas and accept the new and exciting ideas that may be very different from the teacher's own original thoughts.

Experimental design labs include a brainstorming section in which students will discuss and decide on their first design before they begin experimenting. Once students have an idea in mind, they receive their predetermined materials and begin building their ideas. As their ideas are built and tested, students often make modifications to better solve the problem. These modifications are expected and recorded as part of the lab report. The goal of these experiences is to encourage problem solving and thinking out of the box and to reinforce the scientific process. If students have not experienced these types of labs before, they often will be frustrated or worried about its open-ended nature, without an obvious correct result. Students then will seek further clarifications and instructions from the teacher, hoping to build or design what the teacher is seeking. Instead of providing specific instructions or examples, teachers should simply point the students back to the materials and guidelines, reinforcing that there are many different ways to complete the task successfully. Once students truly understand the nature of experimental design, they love the challenge and freedom it encourages and often will ask for more. Almost any lab can be converted to an experimental design experience!

Vocabulary for This Chapter

hypothesis: a testable prediction used to see how something works or to solve a problem

inference: a conclusion drawn based on observations

observation: using your sense to gather information; in science, instruments such as microscopes and balances can be used to carefully gather accurate and detailed observations

problem: a testable scientific question

qualitative: an observation based on physical properties

quantitative: an observation made through measurement or quantities

Lesson 1

Subjects and Skills	Science, Language Arts, Mathematics
Rationale	This activity allows teachers to introduce their preferred lab format and sets a questioning tone for the school year.
Objectives	Students will be able to (1) make qualitative and quantitative observations and (2) distinguish between observations and inferences.

Activity Preparation

1. Prepare your "candle" by using an apple corer to remove approximately a 4–5 cm long cylinder from a raw white potato.
2. Slice a slivered almond very thin and after poking a hole in the top of the potato, place the almond in the top of the potato.
3. Place your "candle" on a baby food jar lid (to give the perception of protecting you from dripping wax).
4. Place 3–4 different wax candles in the front of the classroom. One candle should be off-white and sitting on a baby food jar lid to resemble your "candle." These candles simply help serve as a distraction.

Activity Procedures

1. This activity works best if it is played down as a boring introduction on how to write a lab report. Introduce the lab by stating this will be a pretty straightforward experience of setting up a lab report that will be similar to those used all year, as well as a review of how to make accurate observations.
2. The problem for this lab is: "What is the mystery object?" Of course, you want to make it seem like it isn't a mystery, but a basic lab. Try not to call it a candle.
3. Pick up your "candle" or mystery object, show it to the class and ask students to make a hypothesis that answers the problem. They should also be able to support their idea with at least one reason why they believe it is that object.
4. Discuss your supplies or materials: mystery object, baby food lid, and matches.
5. In order to record procedures, it can be kept fairly simple by simply having students record one or two steps: 1. Observe mystery object. 2. Record observations.
6. The observations for this experience are divided into three phases; therefore students' data tables will need to be divided, as well. Each section will need to be labeled with its title.
7. The first phase is entitled Unlit. Show students the object and ask them to make at least 10 different observations about the mystery object. This is the

opportunity to bring up qualitative and quantitative observations. The object can be weighed and measured. Students may see it closely, but ask them not to touch it, as it is not always appropriate to touch things in a lab to make observations. They may "waft" it and record their findings. Once everyone has 10 observations, proceed to the next phase.

8. The second phase is entitled Lit. Go to the front of the classroom and light the almond. It will burn briefly. Before the almond extinguishes itself, blow it out. Again walk around and have students make observations. The observations can be about the object while it burned, as well as after it was extinguished. (Note: Some students will note that wax melted.)

9. The last phase has no title yet. Explain that this phase is very short and everyone will need to watch carefully. Once everyone is attentive, bite off a piece of the object, crunching loudly, chewing soundly, and swallowing. Eat the rest of the object and show that it is gone. Have students record 5 observations of this phase, entitled Eaten.

10. This is the perfect opportunity to discuss the difference between observations and inferences. Obviously you did not eat wax, so have the students go through their observations and circle any that were really inferences.

11. Students will now need to analyze all of their observations and prepare a new hypothesis. Their hypothesis should be able to be supported by all of their observations (e.g., flammable, crunchy, white).

12. Allow students to have the evening to try and figure out what the mystery object could have been. Although they may quickly figure out that it was a potato, they may not be able to figure out how it burned, as potatoes do not ignite.

13. This is your opportunity to have fun with the students and set the tone for the year. They will talk about the time their teacher ate the candle for years to come.

Materials Needed   Apple corer
                   Baby food jar lids
                   Matches
                   Slivered almonds
                   Raw white potato

Chapter 3

Force and Motion in Newton's Laws

Force and Motion Overview

Forces and motion take place around us constantly. They are part of our daily lives. By studying forces and motions, students will become even more aware of the world around them and have answers to many of the "why" questions that seem to frequently pop into their heads. When discussing forces and motion, students always can provide lots of examples when asked. Depending on their prior instruction, however, they may not know that Newton's Three Laws can define these motions.

Newton's First Law of Motion states than an object will remain in motion or at rest unless acted upon by an outside force. For example, a soccer ball will remain at rest unless it is acted upon by a kick. It also would remain in motion in a straight line until it is acted upon by another force that could be another player, or friction, which would eventually slow it to a stop. This law also is known as Newton's Law of Inertia.

Newton's Second Law of Motion states that an object will accelerate in the direction of the force placed upon it. This acceleration will be directly related to the mass of the object and the force placed upon it. It is associated with the mathematical formula: f=m*a in which f is the force in Newtons, m is the object's mass in Kilograms, and a is the object's acceleration in meters per second. When you use the soccer ball example above, the ball will accelerate in the direction of the force placed upon it by the kicker. It also will accelerate differently based on the amount of force placed upon it.

Newton's Third Law of Motion states that for every action there is an equal and opposite reaction. For example, when a soccer player hits a soccer ball off his or her head, as the head strikes the ball, it presses forward into the ball and the ball presses back with equal force. This law also is considered the law of action-reaction pairs.

Objectives for Force and Motion

By completing the lessons in this chapter, the students will be able to:
- express how forces cause motion;
- identify balanced and unbalanced forces;
- express that friction is the force that opposes motion;
- identify examples of Newton's Three Laws;

- understand that any motion can be defined with Newton's Laws; and
- calculate speed, velocity, and acceleration.

Chapter Activities

Below is an outline of the lessons included in this chapter. Depending on your students' prior knowledge, you can pick which lessons you want to use to reinforce the concepts. I suggest that you start with the project introduction so that all of the information and concepts presented during the class will tie back into the project.

In Lesson 2, the teacher will introduce the rubric and expectations for the Newton In the News project. Newton's Three Laws of Motion constantly are taking place, every second of the day. Not only is motion constantly taking place, but contrary to what most people believe, a motion (say, pushing a key on the computer) can be considered an example of all three laws depending on how you interpret the motion. This project asks students to recognize various examples of the laws and then defend their decisions. This helps the students look at Newton's Laws of Motion in new ways and process them in greater depth. In order for students to have enough time to complete this project, they should have at least 3 weeks to work on it.

Students really enjoy the opportunity to act out concepts. Lesson 3 allows students to work together to pantomime examples of each of Newton's Laws of Motion. After the pantomimes, classmates will guess which law of motion was shown and defend their guesses using definitions and key vocabulary of the three laws.

Supplies and managing equipment can be a problem in the science classroom. By setting up a rotational lab, like those described in Lesson 4, students can have access to materials and equipment, but the teacher only needs one set of equipment. The rotational labs in this activity are card based; all of the instructions should be copied on cards and laminated for durability. These experiences are short and exploratory in nature.

Lesson 5 allows students to look at various sports clips to observe Newton's Laws in action. After observing the clips, students will record examples of the laws, as well as use a little creativity to discuss the impact on the sport if the law was absent.

Students will have a lot of fun with Lesson 6. While learning about Newton's third law, they will be experiencing an experimental design activity in which they will design their own Balloon Racer by manipulating variables that control the speed of a balloon traveling along a string, hoping to create the fastest racer.

Vocabulary for This Chapter

acceleration: the rate at which velocity changes

action-reaction force pairs: a pair of forces that act upon two interacting objects

equilibrium: a state of motion in which two forces are equal to each other and no motion occurs

force: a push or pull one body exerts on another

friction: the forces that opposes motion between two surfaces that are touching each other

inertia: the tendency of an object to resist any change in its motion

mass: a measurement of the amount of matter in an object; its SI unit is the kilogram (kg)

motion: a change in place or position

Newton: a unit for force, equals one kg*m/sec^2

speed: the rate of motion, or the rate at which a body changes position

velocity: a change in direction or a change in speed

Lesson 2

NEWTON IN THE NEWS PROJECT INTRODUCTION

Subjects and Skills	Science, Language Arts
Rationale	This project will allow students the opportunity to discover examples of Newton's Laws in real-world situations, defend their opinions using scientific vocabulary, and use persuasive writing skills.
Objectives	The students will (1) choose appropriate real-world examples of Newton's three laws and (2) defend their choices.
Activity Preparation	1. Collect local newspapers as resources for those students who do not have access to them.
Activity Procedures	1. Give each student a rubric for the Newton in the News project (p. 12).
	2. This project is worth up to 200 points, rather than the usual 100 points, although the grade still can be recorded as a percentage. Discuss each grading criterion with the students, providing examples and explanations for excellent, good, fair, and poor.
	3. After discussing the criteria, depending on remaining time, students are ready to progress to the next activity. Students should work on locating articles and writing their summaries and defenses for each article as the other lessons in this unit are being taught. Students will turn in this project at the end of the unit.
Materials Needed	Newton in the News Rubric (see p. 12) Newspapers

Name: _____ Date: _____

Newton in the News Project Rubric

Criteria	Excellent	Good	Fair	Poor
Articles Nine articles, from the newspaper, no comic strips or magazine/Internet articles	20 *points* All nine articles complete and present; three articles for each law; all from newspaper.	15 *points* Five to eight articles complete and present; two for each law; all from newspaper.	10 *points* One to four articles present; less than two for each law; articles incomplete or from wrong sources.	0 *points* No articles present.
Recentness of Articles Articles must be dated within the past 30 days.	20 *points* All dated within the past 30 days.	15 *points* 75% of articles dated within the past 30 days.	10 *points* 25% of articles dated within the past 30 days.	0 *points* Articles are more than 60 days old.
Summaries Use proper paragraph form; includes one summary paragraph for each article.	50 *points* Summaries complete and present for all articles; accurate in detail and form.	30 *points* Summaries present for all articles; accurate in detail and form; some not completed.	20 *points* Some summaries are missing or those that are submitted are not accurate in form or detail or completed.	0 *points* No summaries present.
Defense of Article Use proper paragraph form; includes one defense paragraph for each article; includes the law represented and the relationship between law and article; uses scientific vocabulary.	50 *points* Defense complete and present for all articles; relates each article to the law it represents; uses proper form and detail; includes scientific vocabulary.	30 *points* Defense complete and present for all articles; not all articles are related to laws; does not include scientific vocabulary.	20 *points* Some defenses are missing; defenses do not include relationship to laws or scientific vocabulary.	0 *points* No defenses present.
Bibliography Follows proper bibliographical format; all articles listed in bibliography.	20 *points* All articles listed; bibliographical format is followed and accurate.	15 *points* 75% of articles are listed; mostly uses proper format.	10 *points* 75% of articles are listed; does not use proper format.	0 *points* 50% or less are listed.
Organization In proper order as follows: article, summary, defense, bibliography.	10 *points* Organized properly; easy to find and read articles.	8 *points* Organized properly, but hard to find and read articles.		0 *points* Unorganized; hard to find and read articles.
Presentation Articles presented creatively.	30 *points* Creative presentation.	20 *points* Basic presentation (e.g., folder).	10 *points* Messy presentation.	0 *points* Very poor presentation overall.

Total Grade: _____
(Out of 200)

Lesson 3

BRINGING NEWTON TO LIFE

Subjects and Skills	Science, Theater Arts/Oral Presentation Skills
Rationale	This activity will allow students to associate body movements with each of Newton's Laws and give students the opportunity to perform in front of their peers.
Objectives	Students will (1) develop motions to show each of Newton's Laws, (2) be able to identify examples of Newton's Laws, and (3) be able to defend their ideas.

Activity Preparation

1. After introducing the concept of motion, discuss that all motions can be defined by Newton's Three Laws of Motion.
2. Have students examine the simple motion of writing on a piece of paper.
3. Ask students which law of motion is demonstrated through this example (students will usually choose the second law, because the pencil is moving in the direction of the force placed upon it).
4. Review the first law of motion: that an object will remain at rest or in motion until acted up on by an outside force. Have students brainstorm how writing on a piece of paper could demonstrate this law. Most will say that the pencil would continue moving until your muscles stop it, or that the pencil would remain at rest (not moving) until it is acted upon by the hand.
5. Next, review the third law of motion. Ask students how writing on a piece of paper demonstrates action-reaction pairs. This law applies as students discover that as the pencil pushes down on the paper or table, the table pushes back.
6. At this point, students should be ready to examine various examples of motion and defend how they show each of Newton's laws.
7. Continue to discuss this in depth and ask students to examine and give several of their own examples.
8. Have students brainstorm and discuss various Charades-like examples of Newton's Three Laws.

Activity Procedures

1. Each group will need to brainstorm three unique hand or body movements (similar to Charades), one for each of Newton's Laws. Students cannot use your examples. Each group will develop their own way of conveying these examples without using any words (sounds and props are encouraged).
2. After reminding students of appropriate behavior while watching and conducting presentations, have each group present their various motions for their classmates.
3. Based on teacher discretion, classmates should now guess which of Newton's Laws was being demonstrated. Guesses must be accompanied by a defense

using scientific terminology that explains why the motion exemplifies the law.

4. Allow multiple groups to present the motions as the audience makes their guesses and defends their responses.

Materials Needed   Props, optional

Lesson 4

ON THE MOVE: MOTION ROTATIONAL LAB

Subjects and Skills Science, Mathematics, Language Arts

Rationale This activity allows students to experience different examples of motion and explain observations by applying their knowledge of Newton's three law of motion.

Objectives Students will be able to (1) make predictions based on prior knowledge, (2) record accurate observations, and (3) using their knowledge of Newton's laws of motion, explain observations made in the rotational labs.

Activity Preparation

1. These labs work well when the procedure is printed for students on large colored index cards (5 x 8) that can be laminated for durability. By setting them up this way, they are easy to spot at the stations, and usually not shuffled in with the students' lab paperwork.

2. Gather the materials for each rotational lab. Set up a station for each lab or buckets with all the supplies that can be taken to student desks.

3. The Egg Test requires two eggs, one raw, one hard-boiled. One needs to be marked with the letter A, the other with a letter B. Make a reference note for yourself as to which letter is the raw egg.

4. To set up the Hero Engine experiment, place an empty aluminum soda can on its side and carefully punch four equally spaced holes around the bottom perimeter of the can using a nail. Place another soda can on its side and carefully punch six equally spaced holes around the bottom. Before removing the nail from each hole, pull the nail slightly, making it parallel to the bottom of the can so all of the holes will be slanted in the same direction. Bend each can's tab up and tie a piece of fishing line to it. Test each can by submerging it in a bucket of water until it is full. Remove the can and allow the water to move out of the holes. The can should begin to spin. If it does not spin well, enlarge the holes slightly until it spins easily. (Note: Once the hero engines are created, they can be stored for future use.)

5. Set up for The Gravity of the Situation lab by obtaining a 2 inch x 2 inch board at least 3 feet long (pine works well). Cut it into six pieces, each with a length of approximately 12 cm long.

6. Decide how the groups will rotate from lab to lab, as free rotations or in a specific order.

Activity Procedures

1. Have students create their own lab sheet by folding one piece of paper into fours. Have them number each square 1–9. (The last lab station number can

go in the top margin of the back page.) Each number represents one of the rotational labs.

2. Instruct students to record their predictions, observations, and questions for each lab in its appropriate square. Before beginning their rotation, students can set up each square of their lab paper to record the information from each station.

3. Briefly explain each station to students. Students can make any specific notes about special tips for success or safety on their lab paper for each station.

4. Break students into groups and allow them to rotate through the stations based on the order you have specified.

5. Collect the students' lab sheets and review their observations.

<table>
<tr><td style="vertical-align:top; width:25%;">Suggestions for the
Motion Mini-Labs</td><td>Here are some suggestions to help the following labs run smoothly in your classroom:

- *Station 1: The Egg Test:* This station has two white eggs, one raw, one hard-boiled. Students will need to use caution when handling them so they do not break or crack.
- *Station 2: The Hero Engine:* Remind students that the engine needs to always be held over the bucket of water.
- *Station 3: Flick a Coin:* Remind students to use care in this station because they are flicking coins, which could create a safety issue if they are careless.
- *Station 4: The Gravity of the Situation:* Remind students that the pieces of wood at this station are not meant to be used as noisemakers, weapons, or swords.
- *Station 5: Newton's Law in a Cup:* Demonstrate the hand movement that needs to be done for this station. It should be a quick turn of the wrist as if you were turning a doorknob. The oil and food coloring do not move even though the cup has.
- *Station 7: The Coin on the Elbow Trick:* Students need to be careful that they are not near other students while trying this station, as pennies have been known to go flying. The trick to succeeding is the use of Newton's First Law—the pennies should not be bumped into the air (as many students will try to do); instead, they should engage inertia and catch the pennies on the way down.</td></tr>
<tr><td style="vertical-align:top;">Materials (for a class
with seven lab groups)</td><td>A book that you don't mind students dropping (hardcover works best)
Bucket or tub of water
Chicken Little or other familiar children's book
Clear plastic cup
Cup or mug
Two empty soda pop cans with tabs
Two eyedroppers
Fishing line
Food coloring
Two white hardboiled eggs</td></tr>
</table>

Index card
Nail or ice pick
10 pennies (but a few more is always handy, as they do sometimes get lost)
Two white raw eggs
Scrap paper
Vegetable oil
Wooden boards (2 inches x 2 inches; 6 lengths cut to approximately 12 cm each)

Materials: Two white eggs, one marked A, one marked B.

Procedure:

1. Examine each egg by looking at it. Predict which egg you think is raw and which is hardboiled. Briefly explain why you have made this prediction.
2. Spin each egg on the table. Be careful not spin the eggs so hard that they break!
3. As you spin each egg, record your observations for each.

Questions:

1. Based on your observations, have your predictions about which egg is hardboiled and which is raw changed? Explain your reasoning.
2. When you spin an egg, which of Newton's Laws is at work? Explain.
3. How can Newton's Laws help you discover which egg is raw? Explain.

Materials: Two hero engines (soda cans) and a bucket of water.

Procedure:

1. Submerge one of the engines in the bucket of water until it is completely filled.
2. Predict what you think will happen when this engine is lifted from the water.
3. Remove the engine from the water by lifting the fishing line.
4. Hold the engine approximately 5–6 cm above the water.
5. Record your observations.
6. Repeat these steps with the other engine.

Questions:

1. What is the difference between the two hero engines? How does this impact the way that they function?
2. This apparatus is called a hero engine, although it does not burn fossil fuels like most engines. Why is this an appropriate name for the apparatus?
3. This engine represents all of Newton's Laws. Explain.

© Prufrock Press • *Hands-On Physical Science*

18   This page may be photocopied or reproduced with permission for student use.

STATION 3: FLICK A COIN

Materials: Six pennies.

Procedure:
1. Make a stack of five pennies on your table.
2. Place the sixth penny on the table approximately 10 cm from the pile of pennies.
3. Discuss what you think will happen if you quickly flick the penny into the penny at the bottom of the pile. Record your prediction.
4. Carefully and quickly flick the penny into the pile. Record your observations.
5. Try using different distances from the pile and speeds of the "flicks."

Questions:
1. How did speed and distance affect your results?
2. Using scientific vocabulary and Newton's Laws, explain your observations.

STATION 4: THE GRAVITY OF THE SITUATION

Materials: Six wood boards.

Procedure:
1. This station centers on trying to solve a problem. There are six boards of equal length at this station. Your goal will be to stack and overlap the boards in such a way that the last board, although supported by the others, will seem to be hanging in midair (it cannot be over the table in any way).
2. Record your thoughts on how this structure could be created.

Questions:
1. Make a drawing of the structure that solved this problem.
2. How is this type of structure used in real-world buildings?
3. Explain how gravity comes into play when solving this problem.

STATION 5: NEWTON'S LAW IN A CUP

Materials: A cup, food coloring, water, vegetable oil, and two eyedroppers.

Procedure:
1. Fill the cup half-full of water.
2. Using an eyedropper, carefully place the oil on top of the water, so it forms a thin layer.
3. Using another eyedropper, place 4 drops of food coloring onto the oil.
4. Predict what will happen to the water, oil, and food coloring when you quickly turn the cup.
5. Grasping the cup from the top, quickly turn the cup, as if you were turning a doorknob.
6. Record your observations.

Questions:
1. Why was the food coloring put on the oil, rather than in the water?
2. This clearly shows ones of Newton's Laws. Which do you feel it best demonstrates? Why?

STATION 6: FALLING OBJECTS

Materials: A book and a piece of scrap paper.

Procedure:
1. Predict what will happen when you drop the paper and the book to the floor at the same time.
2. Trial One: Hold the book and the piece of paper, one in each hand. Release both at the same time from waist height.
3. Record your observations.
4. Trial Two: Predict what will happen if you place the book on top of the paper and drop them both. Try it! Record your observations.
5. Trial Three: Predict what will happen if you reversed the order and put the paper on top of the book before dropping them both. Try this and record your observations.

Questions:
1. What factors affected results in your first trial? Was it what you predicted?
2. How were your results different in Trial Two? What it what you predicted? Explain.
3. Explain your observations for Trial Three. Why did this happen?
4. How is this station related to the value 9.8 m/sec^2?

© Prufrock Press • *Hands-On Physical Science*

20
This page may be photocopied or reproduced with permission for student use.

STATION 7: THE COIN ON THE ELBOW TRICK

Materials: Three pennies.

Procedure:

1. The success of this trick is based on one of Newton's Laws of motion. Bend your arm in such a way that your elbow is in line with your ear, and your forearm is perpendicular to the floor. (The palm of your hand will be facing up and your fingers will be near your ear if you are doing it correctly.)
2. By bending your arm this way, you have created a flat shelf near your elbow, on which you can rest a coin (or a pile of coins if you feel brave).
3. Rest a coin near your elbow.
4. Drop your elbow down, bringing your hand around to catch the coin. (It may take a little practice to master the movement.)
5. Record your observations.

Questions:

1. What method seemed to be most effective for catching the coins?
2. What law of motion is best shown by this station? Explain.

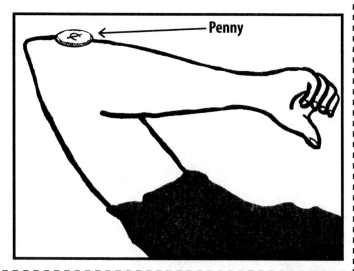

STATION 8: THE COIN, THE CUP, AND THE CARD

Materials: An index card, a plastic cup, and a penny.

Procedure:

1. Place the card on top of the cup.
2. Place the penny on top of the card so that it is over the center of the cup.
3. Predict how the penny will move if the card was flicked away.
4. Carefully flick the card parallel to the table. Record your observations.

Questions:

1. Explain why the penny moved as it did.
2. What two forces acted on the coin?
3. Which law of motion does this station demonstrate? How do you know?

STATION 9: THE SKY IS FALLING!

Materials: A children's book.

Procedure:
1. Children's books are filled with various examples of Newton's Laws.
2. Your challenge is to find at least five examples of each of Newton's Laws in this children's book. Record your examples and how they represent the law you have chosen.

Questions:
1. Any children's book could have been used for this station. Why is this true?
2. Why do you think your teacher chose to use a children's book rather than a novel?

Lesson 5

NEWTON DOES SPORTS

Subjects and Skills	Science, Mathematics, Language Arts
Rationale	This activity will allow students to experience physical concepts at work in the world around them and realize how different the world would be if certain laws did not function as expected.
Objectives	Students will (1) identify examples of Newton's Laws in various sports clips and (2) explain how various sports would be impacted if a certain law ceased to work.

Activity Preparation

1. Briefly review Newton's three laws to confirm that students feel comfortable identifying examples of the laws.
2. Discuss that these laws are constantly happening all around us at all times by having students list three examples of the laws that have taken place in the past 5 minutes.
3. Ask students to brainstorm the impact if one of the laws no longer worked. Have students explain what it might mean if inertia did not exist. How would that impact motion? Allow students to be creative in their responses.

Activity Procedures

1. Distribute the Wide World of Sports Recording Web to students. The front of this paper has a complex web in which students will record specific information. They also will use the back of this page for the preliminary brainstorming phase.
2. Show students the various sports clips. Using the back of the Wide World of Sports Recording Web, students should note specific examples of each law that they observed in the clips.
3. Once they have observed many different video clips of a variety of sports, students should select two sports that interest them most to study further.
4. Using the front of the Wide World of Sports Recording Web, students should first record their two sports in the appropriate spaces.
5. Next, students should discuss how each sport demonstrates the three laws of motion. Students should think about how each law directly impacts the success (or failure) of a participant in the specific sports they selected.
6. Students are now ready to take it to the next level and record on the web how each sport would be impacted if each of Newton's Laws stopped working.

Materials Needed

Video clips of various sports (sports bloopers work well for this)
Wide World of Sports Recording Web (see p. 24)

Name: _____   Date: _____

Wide World of Sports Recording Web

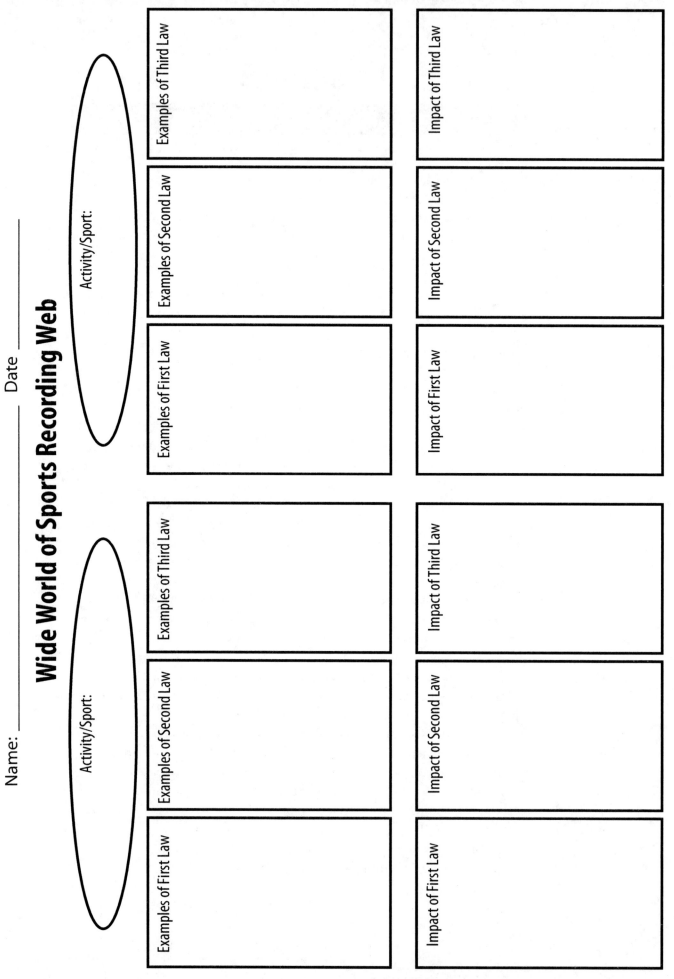

Activity/Sport: _____

| Examples of First Law | Examples of Second Law | Examples of Third Law |

| Impact of First Law | Impact of Second Law | Impact of Third Law |

Activity/Sport: _____

| Examples of First Law | Examples of Second Law | Examples of Third Law |

| Impact of First Law | Impact of Second Law | Impact of Third Law |

Lesson 6

BALLOON RACERS

Subjects and Skills   Science, Language Arts, Mathematics

Rationale   This activity will allow students to experiment with controlled, independent (manipulated) and dependent (responding) variables and experience hands-on examples of everyday physics concepts.

Objectives   Students will (1) identify controlled variables, (2) identify independent and dependent variables, (3) identify action-reaction forces in an experiment, and (4) calculate the speed of a moving object.

Activity Preparation
1. The string racing courses (using string at least 8–10 meters in length) will need to be set up in the classroom so that students have an idea of the length they would like their balloon rocket to travel. This can be set up between two chairs with the string tied securely to one chair, with the other end free so the string can be fed through the straw on the balloon. Once the straw racer has been put on the string, the string will be tied to the other chair for the race, then removed for the next racer.
2. Supplies will need to be grouped in buckets or made available for groups when the activity begins.

Activity Procedures
1. Begin the lab discussion by introducing the concept of experimental design. Reinforce that this experience has many possible results and it is the goal of their group to use certain materials to meet certain guidelines. Everyone's experiment will be different.
2. Discuss the basic construction guidelines. Racers must:
    * use one balloon,
    * have at least one set of fins, and
    * have a straw securely attached so the racer can run the string course.

3. Although this may seem very general, this experience is meant to be investigative and based on trial and error. Students may ask for more clarification and instruction, hoping the teacher will tell them how to be successful. If this happens, encourage the students to think of all of the possibilities that these general guidelines will allow them.
4. Discuss with the large group the different variables of the experiment:
    * type of balloon (long or round)
    * amount of air (diameter of inflated balloon)
    * fins (shape, size, placement, number)

- nose cone (present or not present)
- straw (length of straw, placement on balloon)

5. Briefly instruct or remind students that when conducting an experiment, they only want to manipulate one variable at a time, keeping the others consistent.

6. Explain the safety guidelines for the activity, including:
   - The number of students (or groups) that will be able to race at one time (this will be determined by space and number of strings set up in advance).
   - Students will need to blow up their own balloons, and they should not use any balloons that others have already used.
   - When transporting the balloon racer and preparing to release the air, remind students to try to avoid wrapping the neck of the balloon around their finger. (Fingers can get really red and painful if they wait too long.) Instead they can just twist the neck of the balloon and pinch it closed.
   - Balloons should not be released unless they are on the string and the string is pulled tight and ready for racing.
   - The process for how the test racing will be managed.

7. Allow time for students to brainstorm and create ideas. This can be done on the students' lab reports or the Balloon Racer handout (see pp. 28–32).

8. When students have developed a plan, give each group its supplies. Allow students time to work on building their balloon racer.

9. Students will need to be able to test their balloon racers, record their observations, and using the stopwatches, record their racing times as the air is released from the balloon in a data table as they manipulate their chosen variable to increase their racer's speed. The data table on the brainstorming sheet allows three trials of each manipulation of the variable.

10. Once students have conducted their trials, they can calculate the average speed of their racer for each trial.

11. At this point, everyone is ready for the Balloon Racer Competition, in which each group now submits their best combination of two of the variables they tested, hoping to have the fastest racer.

12. Have each group bring their fastest racer to the course.

13. Time each as the air is released and they speed along the course.

14. Have students record their times on their data table as the balloons race along the string and using the length of the string for the distance, calculate the speeds of their racers.

Materials Needed   For each group:

Balloons of different shapes and sizes

Drinking straws

Tape

Ruler

Scissors

Index cards (for fins)

String and a ruler or measuring tape (to measure the diameter of the filled balloon)

Stopwatch

For teacher:

String for the race tracks (at least 8–10 meters for each track)

Stopwatch

Name: _____ Date: _____

Balloon Racers

In this experiment, you will be working with Newton's Third Law, which focuses on action-reaction pairs. By experimenting and manipulating two variables, your group will be trying to create a Balloon Racer that will reach the end of the racecourse in the least amount of time as the air is released from the balloon.

BASIC CONSTRUCTION GUIDELINES FOR YOUR BALLOON RACER

Each balloon racer must:
- use one balloon,
- have at least one set of fins, and
- have a straw securely attached so it can run the string course.

Possible variables to test include:
- type of balloon (long or round);
- amount of air (diameter of inflated balloon);
- fins (shape, size, placement, number);
- nose cone (present or not present); and
- straw (length of straw, placement on balloon).

MATERIALS AVAILABLE

- 1 long balloon
- 1 round balloon
- 4 drinking straws
- Index cards (for fins)
- Ruler
- String and ruler or measuring tape (measure diameter of filled balloon)
- Stopwatch
- Tape
- Scissors

VARIABLE (HYPOTHESIS) STATEMENT

What is the first variable your group will test? How do you think this variable will affect the performance your Balloon Racer? Why do you think this? What variables will you control?

_____

_____

_____

_____

_____

Name: _____ Date: _____

What is the second variable your group will test? How do you think this variable will affect the performance your Balloon Racer? Why do you think this? What variables will you control?

_____

_____

_____

_____

CONSTRUCTION PLANS/BRAINSTORMING

Use this space to record or brainstorm construction ideas for your Balloon Racer.

Name: _____ Date: _____

Test your two chosen variables, recording your findings in the charts below.

Variable 1: _____

Variables	Trial 1 (sec)	Trial 2 (sec)	Trial 3 (sec)	Average Time (sec)	Distance Traveled (m)	Average Speed (m/sec)

Variable 2: _____

Variables	Trial 1 (sec)	Trial 2 (sec)	Trial 3 (sec)	Average Time (sec)	Distance Traveled (m)	Average Speed (m/sec)

What combination of your two variables will produce the fastest run? Use your data to support your response.

_____

_____

_____

Name: _____ Date: _____

Write your chosen procedure for developing your Balloon Racer on the lines below. Remember to be very specific about the steps you took to construct your Balloon Racer. Use enough detail and measurements that someone else could recreate your racer!

_____

_____

_____

_____

_____

_____

Draw your final design in the box below.

Name: _____ Date: _____

Time to test your prediction! As each racer participates, complete the data table below with their speeds.

Balloon Racer Group Number	Trial 1 (sec)	Trial 2 (sec)	Trial 3 (sec)	Average Time (sec)	Distance Traveled (m)	Average Speed (m/sec)

Balloon racing is an example of Newton's Third Law of Motion. Using scientific vocabulary, explain why this is an example of the third law.

_____

_____

_____

_____

_____

_____

_____

Chapter 4

Energy and Heat

When discussing energy and heat, students cannot help but note all of the "unit scientists." Many of the units (Watts, Joules, Newtons, etc.) come from the names of famous scientists who developed or furthered various scientific studies. Therefore, this unit is centered on a famous scientist product. This product asks students to research a specific scientist, create a presentation that displays why he or she is considered famous, present their information to their peers, and provide positive feedback to their peers.

In this unit, students will study the various types of energy and their sources, from energy from the sun (solar), to energy made from the heat of the earth (geothermal). Students will investigate potential or stored energy and its conversion into kinetic or energy in motion. This conversion is part of the Law of Conservation of Energy that states that energy cannot be created nor destroyed, but simply converted into other forms.

They also will investigate work. Work is measured in joules (named for James Joule) and only takes place when a force is moved through a distance, such as pushing a book along a desk or lifting a backpack from the floor. Work can be calculated using the mathematical formula: $W = F*d$ (Work = Force in Newtons multiplied by the distance in meters). Once students understand work, they can easily move on to study power. Power is measured in Watts (names for James Watt) and is the amount of work that can be completed in a certain amount of time. Power is calculated using the formula: $P = W/t$ (Power measured in Watts is equal to the amount of Work done in joules divided by the amount of time, usually in seconds, it took to complete the work).

Students also will get to experience the difference between a calorie (small calorie) and a Calorie (large calorie). These two words often are confused, because the only written difference is the capital C. In physics, there actually is a significant difference between these two words—a factor of one thousand to be exact. Physically speaking, a calorie is the amount of energy it takes to change 1 gram of water, 1 degree Celsius, while a Calorie (large calorie) is 1,000 small calories. Students are familiar with the word calorie and quickly will associate it with food. Calories are a measure of energy. The Calories found in food are actually large Calories or 1,000 small calories. For example, when looking at a small package of cut apples, the nutritional information states 40 Calories. This would equate to 40,000 small calories. The nutritional labels would suddenly need a lot more space if we recorded the number of calories! There are some food products, usually energy bars, that do strive to list their nutritional information in a complete and "correct" way; instead of just listing calories on their labels, they record kilocalories. This is another correct way to report the number of Calories. Although this small detail may seem confusing, as long as students understand that there are two different kinds of calories, one being 1,000 times bigger than the other, they will better understand how to calculate the amount of calories in food.

Objectives for Energy and Heat

By completing the lessons in this chapter, the students will be able to:
- identity and give examples of potential and kinetic energy,
- identify examples of work and power,
- identify different energy sources,
- distinguish heat from temperature, and
- calculate the amount of calories in food items.

Chapter Activities

Below is a list of the lessons included in this chapter. Depending on the prior knowledge of your students, you can choose which activities you prefer to use to reinforce the concepts. I always suggest that you start with the project introduction so that all of the information and concepts presented during the class will tie back into the project.

In Lesson 7, the teacher will introduce the rubric and expectation for the Famous Scientist Project. This project has four parts: the research, the PowerPoint presentation, the oral presentation, and the Hall of Fame proposal paper. An anticipation guide is a quiz given to students before they have had any formal contact with the information. The anticipation guide in Lesson 8 asks students some seemingly obvious questions, with perhaps some unexpected answers.

Venn diagrams allow students the opportunity to compare and contrast different ideas, in this case, various energy sources with which students may not be as familiar. Lesson 9 allows students to compare two of the following energy sources: fossil fuels, geothermal, wind, solar, nuclear, tidal, hydropower, and biomass.

One of the best examples of the continuous energy exchange between potential and kinetic energy is a roller coaster. Lesson 10 allows students to observe this energy exchange, as well as practice their scientific skills as they complete an experiment design experience that asks them to create a successful roller coaster for a "marble" car.

Students are familiar with the idea that machines use power to do work, but do humans use power? You bet! Lesson 11 has students calculate the power they use to climb a set of stairs in Watts, horsepower, and kilowatts. The teacher-directed, student-performed demonstrations in Lesson 12 are intended to show the concepts of heat and conductivity, keeping safety in mind.

A Calorie is a measure of energy that can be found in food. In Lesson 13, students build a simple calorimeter, then test and calculate the calories (or food energy) in a peanut and a marshmallow. Students also can test other foods.

After researching their famous scientists, students will present their information to their peers using the guidelines in Lesson 14. The audience will have the opportunity to give positive feedback to the presenter through feedback forms shared after the presentations.

Vocabulary for This Chapter

biomass: energy obtained through organic materials, such as plant material, vegetation, or agricultural waste

Calorie: 1,000 small calories, or the amount of heat required to raise the temperature of 1 kilogram of water 1 degree Celsius

calorie: a unit of heat, equal to the amount of heat required to raise the temperature of 1 gram of water 1 degree Celsius

Hands-On Physical Science

conduction: the transfer of energy through matter in which energy moves from particle to particle

convection: the transfer of energy by the bulk movement of matter in which particles move from place to place in a fluid

fossil fuels: fuels formed from the remains of plants and animals that lived millions of years ago

geothermal: energy produced by the heat inside the earth

heat: thermal energy that flows from a warmer material to a cooler material

hydroelectric power: power created by harnessing the energy of flowing water, often through the use of dams

joules: the basic unit of energy and work, named for English scientist, James Prescott Joule; 1 joule (j) = a force of 1 Newton moving through 1 meter

kinetic energy: energy in the form of motion

Law of Conservation of Energy: a law stating that that energy can change form but cannot be created or destroyed under ordinary conditions

Newton: the basic unit of force, named for Isaac Newton; 1 Newton (N) is equal to the force that produces an acceleration of 1 meter per second per second on a mass of one kilogram

nuclear power: power created from the energy stored in an atomic nucleus, specifically, nuclear fission or fusion

potential energy: stored energy

power: the amount of work that can be done within a certain amount of time; usually measured in Watts

radiation: the transfer of energy in the form of waves

solar energy: energy from the sun

specific heat: the amount of energy needed to raise the temperature of 1 kg of a material 1 K; it is measured in joules per kilogram per Kelvin

temperature: a measure of the average kinetic energy of the particles that make up a specific sample of matter

thermal energy: total energy of a material's particles, including both kinetic (vibrations and movements within and between particles) and potential energy (resulting from forces that act within and between particles

tidal energy: energy created by exploiting the rise and fall in sea levels due to the tides

Watts: the basic unit of power named for James Watt; 1 Watt (W) is equal to the amount of power created by 1 joule of work being completed in 1 second

wind energy: energy created by using the wind to turn windmills and turbines

work: the transfer of energy through motion; work is equal to the force exerted multiplied by the distance moved; usually measured in joules

Lesson 7

WHAT MAKES A SCIENTIST FAMOUS? PROJECT

Subjects and Skills   Science, Language Arts, History, Technology

Rationale   This project will allow students the opportunity to understand the impact one person can have on science and allow them to use their public speaking skills.

Objectives   Students will (1) research a scientist to discover what made him or her famous and (2) create a PowerPoint presentation to enhance an oral report.

Activity Preparation

1. Make arrangements for access to computers, usually for 2–3 days throughout the unit in order for students to create their PowerPoint presentations.
2. Decide how the research will be conducted. Once this has been decided, time in the library or additional computer time will be needed for research within the first week of the unit. If you choose to use Internet research, choose Web sites that the students can use to research their scientists.
3. Choose the scientists that students will research. Although a scientist may be a household name (like Celsius), there is sometimes not a lot of information readily available for him or her.
4. Write the names of the scientists on slips of paper or cards.

Activity Procedure

1. As each student enters the classroom, have him or her choose one of the cards or slips of paper with a scientist's name.
2. Give each student a rubric for the famous scientist project and have him or her record his or her scientist's name on the rubric.
3. Discuss the grading scale with students. The project is worth up to 200 points, rather than the usual 100 points, although the grade can still be recorded as a percentage. Discuss each criterion with the students, providing examples and explanations for excellent, good, fair, and poor columns. Discuss with students how they will be conducting their research and how they should record their findings and sources.
4. Students now are ready to begin their research.

Materials Needed   Microsoft PowerPoint or other presentation software
Famous Scientist Rubric (see pp. 37–38)
Famous Scientists List (see p. 39)
Cards or slips of paper

Name: _____ Date: _____

Famous Scientist Presentation Project Rubric

Your Scientist: _____

Criteria	Excellent	Good	Fair	Poor
Title Page	15 *points* Includes scientist's name, presenter's name, and at least one picture demonstrating scientist's fame.	10 *points* Includes scientist's name, presenter's name; picture does not demonstrate reason for fame.	5 *points* Includes just scientist's name and presenter's name.	0 *points* No title page present.
Pictures Includes at least two pictures.	25 *points* Includes two pictures: one representing fame and one of student's choice. Choices are good and significant.	15 *points* Includes two pictures: one representing fame and one of student's choice. Not necessarily the best choices.	5 *points* Includes two pictures: one representing fame and one of student's choice. Purpose unclear for choice.	0 *points* One or no pictures present.
Timeline Includes significant events; shows dates after scientist's death with contributions to future.	20 *points* Includes at least seven significant events; shows scientist's contribution after death.	10 *points* Includes at least six significant events; does not show scientist's contribution after death.	5 *points* Includes less than six significant events; does not show scientist's contribution after death.	0 *points* No timeline present.
Evidence of Fame Fame is obvious and explained throughout all aspects of the presentations (words, pictures, speech).	20 *points* Evidence of scientist's fame present and explained throughout presentation.	10 *points* Experiments are discussed, but slideshow does not support evidence for fame as strongly as oral presentation.	5 *points* Some evidence for the scientist's fame is discussed or included in the presentation.	0 *points* Evidence of fame is not apparent.
Slide Requirement Number of slides required, includes title page.	15 *points* Includes 10 or more slides.	10 *points* Includes 7–9 slides.	5 *points* Includes 5–7 slides.	0 *points* Less than 5 slides included.
Rubric	10 *points* Student turns in rubric at time of presentation.			0 *points* Student does not return rubric.
Timing and Flow Presentation flows with speaker; speaker has few pauses; little "dead time."	20 *points* Presentation is timed well; flows with speaker; speaker has few pauses.	10 *points* Presentation is timed fairly well; flows somewhat with speaker; speaker has several pauses.	5 *points* Presentation is not timed well; speaker has frequent pauses.	0 *points* Student has not made the attempt to time his or her presentation with speech.
Presentation Content	15 *points* Presentation covered major contributions of scientist.	10 *points* Presentation missing one key fact or discovery.	5 *points* Presentation has ambiguous or unnecessary facts.	0 *points* Presentation has blatant inaccuracies.

Name: _____ Date: _____

Criteria	Excellent	Good	Fair	Poor
Prop Must be three-dimensional item brought from home related to scientist's fame.	10 *points* Brings three-dimensional item related to scientist's fame.	5 *points* Brings three-dimensional item, but not exactly related to scientist's fame.		0 *points* No prop of any sort or prop is not three-dimensional.
Two Word Rule No more than two words per page, including acronyms, symbols for words, or rebuses. Title page may have more than two words.	20 *points* No pages with more than two words, including acronyms, symbols, or rebuses.	10 *points* One page with more than two words, or the use of an acronym, symbol, or rebus to represent a word.		0 *points* Two or more slides with two or more words, including acronyms, symbols, or rebuses.
Persuasive Essay Should address why the scientist is famous and give documented support for why he or she should be included in a "Scientific Hall of Fame." Must be turned in with rubric on day of presentation.	30 *points* Essay gives three documented scientific reasons and makes a strong argument for scientist's inclusion; double-spaced, typed, includes bibliography.	20 *points* Essay gives at least one documented scientific reason and makes an argument for scientists inclusion; double-spaced, typed, includes bibliography.	10 *points* Essay does not give any documented scientific reasons and/or makes a weak argument for scientist's inclusion; or essay is not in the correct format.	0 *points* Essay is not turned in or information is plagiarized.

Total Grade: _____
(Out of 200)

Famous Scientists List

Marie Curie	Daniel Bernoulli
Anders Celsius	William Thomson Kelvin
James Joule	James Chadwick
Alessandro Volta	Gabriel Daniel Fahrenheit
Pierre Curie	George Simon Ohm
Henri Becquerel	Enrico Fermi
Humphry Davy	Dmitri Mendeleev
Niels Bohr	Democritus
Archimedes	Michael Faraday
John Dalton	Robert Boyle
Henry G. J. Moseley	Antoine Lavoisier
Lise Meitner	Robert Bunsen
Wilhelm Konrad Röntgen	Ernest Rutherford
Julius Lothar Meyer	James Watt
Ole Rømer	Joseph John Thomson

Lesson 8

Subjects and Skills	Science
Rationale	This activity will allow the students to preview the concepts in this unit, form questions about the material, and assess prior knowledge about energy and heat.
Objectives	The student will (1) demonstrate his or her prior knowledge about heat and energy.
Activity Preparation	1. Explain to students that the anticipation guide is not going to be assessed for correctness; its main purpose to see what they already know.
Activity Procedures	1. Distribute the anticipation guide and have students complete the guide by deciding if a statement is true or false. If they think it is false, they should write a brief explanation why they believe this.
	2. After everyone is finished, collect the anticipation guides and begin instruction on the unit itself.
	3. At the end of the unit, return the guides to the students and allow them to make any changes to their original thoughts. This makes a great discussion tool right before the assessment and also serves as a study guide that can be taken home.
Materials Needed	Anticipation Guide (p. 41)
Anticipation Guide Answers	1. False. A rock sitting on a hill does have energy. It has potential energy. Students will investigate potential energy and energy conversions through the experimental design experience where they create their own roller coaster.
	2. True. A rock rolling down a hill has energy. It has kinetic energy. Students will identify examples of kinetic energy through the roller coaster experience.
	3. False. A peanut contains more energy than a marshmallow. Students will use a calorimeter to compare these two foods. The peanut burns for a lot longer and has more calories as calculated by the experiment.
	4. False. All metals conduct heat, but not all of them conduct heat in the same way. Students will be exposed to this concept during the heat demonstrations.
	5. False. Temperature actually is the measure of the kinetic energy of the particles of the substance. This concept is introduced in this chapter through the heat demonstrations and further discussed in the next chapter.

Anticipation Guide

Read each of the following statements. Decide if the statement is true or false. If it is true, record a T on the line, if it is false, record an F. If you think the statement is false, briefly note why you believe it is false.

1. _____ A rock sitting on a hill does not have energy.

2. _____ A rock rolling down a hill has energy.

3. _____ A marshmallow contains more energy than a peanut.

4. _____ All metals conduct heat well.

5. _____ Temperature is a measure of how cold or warm an object may be.

Lesson 9

Subjects and Skills	Science, Language Arts
Rationale	This activity will allow students to use their critical thinking skills, and compare and contrast the benefits and considerations of various energy sources.
Objectives	The students will (1) use a Venn diagram to compare and contrast various energy sources.
Activity Preparation	1. Students will need to have access to various informational resources (Internet, books, etc.) on different energy sources.
	2. If this is the first folded Venn diagram students have created, it is best to have an example prepared that demonstrates how to fold and label the paper.
	3. Based on teacher discretion, students can choose the two energy sources that most interest them (fossil fuels, geothermal, wind, solar, nuclear, tidal, hydro-electric, and biomass).
Activity Procedures	1. Students will need to fold a standard piece of paper in half lengthwise ("hotdog style"). Do not unfold the paper.
	2. Students then will fold the paper into three equal sections, and unfold so they can see the three sections of the paper.
	3. With the fold of the paper to the top, students can now draw a Venn diagram on the front (see Figure 1).

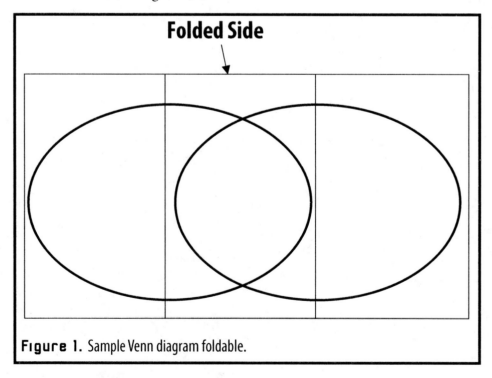

Folded Side

Figure 1. Sample Venn diagram foldable.

4. Now students are ready to investigate their two energy sources, focusing on the following aspects: the benefits and drawbacks of using each source; how each source produces energy (what is required, any byproducts); the effectiveness or efficiency of each method of producing energy; and how the two sources they have chosen are similar and different.

5. Once students have completed their investigations, they are ready to complete their Energy Sources Venn diagram. Students should label the top of the right flap with one of their energy sources and the top of the left with the other. The center or overlapping part of the circle is left unlabeled.

6. There are now many options for the students as they record their research on the diagram. The only restrictions they have in entering their information are the center or overlapping flap of the diagram. This area on the front and inside is reserved for the commonalities between the two energy sources.

Materials Needed   white paper

Lesson 10

A Wild Ride!

Subjects and Skills	Science, Language Arts, Mathematics
Rationale	This activity will allow students to experiment with controlled, independent (manipulated) and dependent (responding) variables and experience a hands-on example of the law of conservation of energy.
Objectives	Students will show the law of conservation of energy by (1) constructing a roller coaster that can safety transport a marble through various loops and (2) identifying the areas of potential and kinetic energy on their roller coaster.

Activity Preparation

1. Review the concepts of potential and kinetic energy.
2. Ask students to provide everyday examples of both potential and kinetic energy. As students share their examples, ask them if their example only demonstrates potential or kinetic energy.
3. Draw a diagram of a rock on the edge of a cliff. Ask students what type of energy is being shown (potential). In fact, the energy level of the rock at the moment is 100% potential. If the rock falls off the cliff, how does its energy change? When would it be 100% kinetic? (Right before it hits the ground and becomes potential again.) Have students share what is happening as the rock falls (the energy is converting from potential to kinetic).
4. Discuss the wording of the Law of Conservation of Energy. Ask students to explain how the falling rock demonstrates this law.
5. Have students share other everyday examples in which the Law of Energy Conservation and energy changes are visible.
6. Prepare the insulation tubes by cutting them lengthwise to create open tracks for the marbles.
7. Review the steps of the scientific process and the idea of controlling one variable at a time while conducting various trials.

Activity Procedures

1. If students have experienced roller coasters, have them share what they enjoy most about the rides and what makes a roller coaster popular or enjoyable.
2. Show students a brief video clip of a high-speed roller coaster. Discuss what they notice about the riders at various points in the ride and how these observations are related to energy changes.
3. Introduce the roller coaster challenge: Can you construct a roller coaster that has at least two hills, one full loop, and one tunnel that gets its marble passenger safely to the cup on the ground?

4. Begin the lab discussion by introducing the concept of experimental design. Reinforce that this experience has many possible results and it is the goal of the groups to use certain materials to meet certain guidelines. Everyone's experiment will be different.

5. Students now can brainstorm ideas for their roller coaster construction. Once they have decided on a design that they feel will solve the problem, they can begin constructing the roller coaster.

6. After various trials, students should develop a coaster that meets all of the criteria and safely gets the marble to the cup at the end.

7. After developing a successful coaster, students will need to record the successful design with measurements of heights at various points, as well as areas of 100% potential and 100% kinetic energies.

Materials Needed (per group)

Cup to catch the marble
Foam pipe insulation for the roller coaster tunnel (one 8-inch piece)
Marble
Meter stick or ruler
Outdoor foam pipe insulation (six tubes, 6 feet in length, cut in half lengthwise)
Tape (to hold foam pipe insulation together)
A Wild Ride handout (pp. 46–47)

Name: _____ Date: _____

A Wild Ride

Can your group construct a roller coaster that has at least two hills, one full loop, and one tunnel that gets its marble passenger safely to the ground?

MATERIALS AVAILABLE (PER GROUP)

- six tubes of 6 foot outdoor foam pipe insulation, cut in half lengthwise
- one 8-inch piece of foam pipe insulation for the roller coaster tunnel
- a marble
- a cup for catching the marble
- tape (to hold insulation together)
- a meter stick/ruler

CONSTRUCTION PLANS/BRAINSTORMING QUESTIONS

1. When designing your roller coaster, what are your biggest considerations?

_____

_____

_____

_____

_____

_____

2. When designing your roller coaster, which features should be placed near the beginning? Why?

_____

_____

_____

_____

_____

_____

3. Brainstorm construction ideas for your roller coaster on the back of this page or a separate sheet of paper.

Name: _____ Date: _____

Record your final design, with all appropriate measurements. Label areas where potential and kinetic energy are at their highest.

Explain how your group's roller coaster design demonstrates the Law of Conservation of Energy.

_____

_____

_____

_____

_____

_____

Lesson 11

HUMAN POWER LAB

Subjects and Skills	Science, Mathematics, Language Arts
Rationale	This activity will allow students to experience everyday physics concepts.
Objectives	Students will (1) calculate the amount of power they expend by climbing stairs, and (2) identify what impacts the amount of power an object can use.

Activity Preparation

1. Choose the staircase that will be used for the experiment. It should have a handrail and be wide enough for two or three students to run up at the same time.
2. Discuss considerations for running up the stairs in a safe manner.
3. Review the factors that impact power: work (force, distance) and time.
4. Decide if this lab will be conducted in groups or individually, keeping in mind that the student who is "working" will need to know their weight or be willing to be weighed for the calculations.

Activity Procedures

1. In order to calculate the power needed to move up the stairs, students will need to find the force, distance, and time. The Human Power Lab sheet goes through the steps used to calculate power.
2. Have students measure the total height of the staircase (distance). The force for each student will be different as it is based on weight. Have the volunteer runner for each group record his or her weight and convert it to Newtons (1 pound = 4.448 Newtons).
3. Once the force and distance have been recorded, students can calculate the amount of work required to move up the stairs. Work is force multiplied by distance, so students will take their weight in Newtons and multiple it by the height of the staircase. The time it takes to run up the stairs will need to be recorded in seconds. These results can then be used to calculate the amount of power (Power = Work/Time) it takes to move up the stairs.
6. Students then have the option of calculating the amount of horsepower and kilowatts they exerted while climbing the stairs.
7. Once students have completed the experience, they should write a conclusion summarizing the lab and addressing any further questions.

Materials Needed

Stopwatch
Meter stick (way to measure height of staircase)
Human Power Lab sheet (pp. 49–50)
Scale

Name: _____ Date: _____

Human Power Lab

Determine the amount of power you create in order to move up a flight of stairs.

1. Record your weight in pounds: _____ lbs.

2. Convert your weight in pounds to Newtons (1 pounds = 4.448 Newtons)

    _____ lbs. x _____ = _____ N.

3. My present weight (based on gravity) is _____ Newtons. This is the force acting upon me.

4. Measure the height of the staircase from the group level to the top of the stairs:

    _____ meters. This is the distance that work will be done.

5. In order to calculate the work completed by climbing the stairs, you must multiple the force exerted by the distance it is moving.

    Force (Newtons) x Distance (meters) = Work (joules)

    _____ Newtons x _____ meters = _____ joules

6. When your timer is ready, run or walk from the bottom of the stairs to the top.

    Record your time in seconds: _____ seconds.

7. In order to calculate the amount of power required to complete your journey up the stairs, you will need to divide the work you did by the amount of time it took

    Work (joules)/time (seconds) = Power (Watts)

    _____ joules / _____ seconds = _____ Watts

EXTENSION CALCULATIONS

You can also figure out how much horsepower you exerted, as well as how many kilowatts of power were used. In order to calculate both of these quantities, use the following ratios:

750 watts = 1 horsepower

1000 watts = 1 kilowatt

I used _____ horsepower.

Using the Internet or library resources, research what types of machines or household objects measure their power in horsepower. Name one object that uses approximately the same amount of horsepower that you used to climb the stairs.

_____

_____

_____

_____

_____

I used _____ kilowatts.

What types of machines or household objects measure their power in kilowatts? Look around your home. Name one object that uses approximately the same amount of kilowatts that you used to climb the stairs.

_____

_____

_____

_____

_____

Lesson 12

HEAT DEMONSTRATIONS

Subjects and Skills	Science
Rationale	This activity allows students to participate in various experiments and discuss their thoughts on discrepant events.
Objectives	The students will identify (1) that different materials conduct heat at different rates and (2) warm fluids rise, while cold fluids sink.

Activity Preparation

1. Set up the Heat Race corks by cutting a piece of bare copper wire to a length of 10 cm. Push it completely through one of the corks from top to bottom. Then, cut two pieces of copper wire approximately 4 cm in length. Push each into opposite ends of the cork, but do not allow them to touch in the middle.
2. Arrange your classroom so that all students will be able to see the demonstrations and come forward when it is their turn to be involved in the demonstration.
3. Discuss safety procedures, and provide safety goggles for teacher, demonstrators, and audience.

Activity Procedures

1. Have students put on their goggles and approach the demonstration table.
2. Using the Teacher Procedures for Heat Demonstrations (see pp. 53–56) and student response sheet (see pp. 57–58), choose the demonstrations you would like to conduct.
3. Before beginning each demonstration, have students record their predictions about what they might observe and why they are making that prediction.
4. After conducting each demonstration, have various students share what they predicted and whether the experience provided answers to their predictions.

Materials Needed

Two index cards
Balloon
Blender (or electric hand mixer)
Candle
Conductometer
Flask (or small mouthed glass bottle)
Food coloring
Four identical, clear glass drinking bottles
Glass rod
Glass tubing or sturdy clear straw
Knitting needle

Matches

Open flame (alcohol burner, Bunsen burner, or candle)

Rigid, bare copper wire

Thermometer

Two corks without center holes

Wire cutters

Teacher Procedures for
Heat Demonstrations

KNITTING NEEDLE VS. THE GLASS ROD

1. Drip a few melted drops of wax onto both the knitting needle and the glass rod about 1 inch from their tips. Allow drops to harden.
2. Ask students to predict which drop of wax will melt first when heated. Have them record their predictions in complete sentences on their Student Note sheets.
3. Hold the ends (nearest the wax drops) over the heat source.
4. As the metal and glass heat, the wax heats. Wait until one of the wax droplets melt and fall.
5. Ask students to explain the reasoning behind their observations.

MOVING WATER

1. Acquire four identical clear small glass bottles with small mouths.
2. Place food coloring into two of the bottles (these will contain the hot water).
3. Fill one of the bottles without food coloring with room temperature water.
4. Fill one of the bottles that contains food coloring with heated water (just below boiling) and cover the mouth of the bottle with an index card.
5. Using a heat resistant glove, invert the bottle of hot water on top of the bottle containing the cooler tap water.
6. Have students predict what will happen when the index card is removed.
7. Carefully remove the card between the bottles.
8. Do the same thing but in opposite order with the cooler bottle on top of the hotter one.
9. Based on the idea that warmer fluids have higher kinetic energy, and are therefore less dense, they will rise above cooler fluids. No matter how the bottles are placed, the warmer colored water will always be in the upper bottle, while the cooler clear water will always end up in the bottom bottle.

THE HEAT RACE

1. Obtain the heat race corks made before the lesson.
2. Have two volunteers come to the demonstration table.
3. After showing the audience the two corks you have prepared, ask the class to predict which person will be able to hold the end of their wire in the flame the longest. (You know the secret, but have the audience explain the reasons for their predictions.) Have students record their predictions on their lab sheets.

4. Give each student one of the prepared corks.

5. Have each student hold one end of the wire while placing the other end in the open flame at the exact same time. Tell him or her that when it is getting too warm to simply drop it.

6. Obviously, the results will be different than what the students expect. They usually will predict that the shorter wire will heat up faster (which it normally would, except ours does not go completely through the cork); instead in our experiment, the longer wire heats up more quickly.

7. Ask students to make various hypotheses that could explain this seemingly incorrect observation. As various ideas are discussed, have other students provide evidence that supports or refutes their classmates' ideas.

8. It usually works best to wait until the next day to share the secret. Students can then brainstorm and develop new ideas to bring to class the next day.

THE CANDLE SNUFFER

1. Make a candle snuffer out of stiff, bare copper wire by twirling the wire into a small cone shape. Four or five twirls should be about right to make the snuffer.

2. Have students predict what will happen when the snuffer is put onto the flame and then removed.

3. Using a lit candle, slowly lower the snuffer onto the flame. (It should go out briefly.)

4. As you lift the snuffer, the flame will return.

5. Brainstorm with students the cause for this phenomenon. (The copper wire becomes the same temperature as the flame, so although it looks like the flame has disappeared; it really has not gone out. It still has access to oxygen and begins burning as soon as the snuffer is removed.)

RISING AND SINKING COLUMNS

1. Fill a clear flask about half full with colored water.

2. Seal the top with a rubber stopper containing glass tubing that goes down into the liquid (see Figure 2 at right).

3. You can create your own flask setup by using a clear glass bottle with a narrow opening filled about half full with colored water. Hold a sturdy clear straw in the mouth of the bottle so that one end of the straw is in the liquid (but not touching the bottom of the bottle) and the other end is sticking out of the top of the bottle. Carefully press the clay around the outside of the

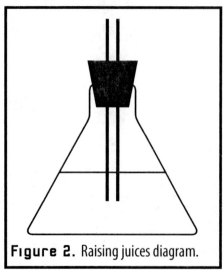

Figure 2. Raising juices diagram.

straw as it passes through the top of the bottle. The clay should hold the straw upright, as well as seal off the bottle.

4. Place the flask or bottle into a pan (to catch the water).
5. Have students predict what will happen when hot water is poured over the flask.
6. Pour hot water over the flask.
7. Have students discuss why the water responds as it does.
8. Have students predict what will happen if ice water is poured over the flask.
9. Pour ice-cold water over the flask.
10. Have students discuss why the water responds differently this time.
11. As in the Moving Water Demonstration (p. 53), as fluids (gas or liquid) heat, the kinetic energy of their molecules increases. As the energy increases, the molecules begin to move and expand. Therefore, as the flask is exposed to hot water, the fluid inside expands because it has more energy; conversely, as the fluid cools, the energy is lowered and the fluid contracts.

Hot Air Balloon

1. Place an empty flask or small-mouthed glass bottle into a pan of water.
2. Place a balloon over the mouth of the flask or bottle.
3. Have students predict what will happen when the water in the pan is heated.
4. Heat the water.
5. Have students record their observations.
6. Again, the teacher can expect the balloon to expand as the fluids heat inside the flask and begin to expand.

Conductometer

1. A conductometer is a flower-shaped tool with congruent "petals" made from six different metals. It is a very inexpensive piece of equipment available from most science supply catalogs. If you do not have one, you can create one by using equal length and gauge wires or rods of different metals. Most conductometers use aluminum, brass, nickel, stainless steel, copper, and iron.
2. Place a drop of wax on the ends of each of the conductometer metals.
3. Ask the students to predict which wax droplet will melt first. This would be a good time to bring in the specific heat values for these metals if you need to cover this concept.
4. Hold the center of the conductometer over the flame (or hold the different metals in the flame and time each melting process).
5. Carefully watch the various drops of wax.
6. Record the order in which the drops of wax melt and drip from each metal.
7. Students are now ready to brainstorm explanations for their observations.

8. Depending on the metals in the conductometer, the wax will melt at different times based on the specific heat of each metal. Specific heat is a measure of how much energy it takes to change one gram of a substance one degree Celsius. Therefore, the lower the specific heat, the less the energy needed to change one gram of that substance. Most conductometers have an instruction sheet that includes the specific heat of each metal.

BLENDED WATER

1. Place approximately 200 mL of room temperature water in a blender.
2. Record the temperature of the water.
3. Have students predict what will happen if the water is blended.
4. Blend the water for 3–4 minutes.
5. Quickly take the temperature of the water again.
6. Have students recall the Law of Conservation of Energy—that energy is never lost or gained, but can be transformed. (Students experienced the transformation between kinetic and potential energy in the roller coaster lab.)
7. Ask students how this demonstration is an example of this law. They should be able to state where the energy was created (the blender) and what transformation took place (transfer to the water). By using the blender, the energy from the blades was transferred to the water. The higher temperature is evidence of this energy transfer.

Student Notes: Heat Demonstrations

Answer the following questions on your own piece of paper.

KNITTING NEEDLE VS. THE GLASS ROD

1. What is your prediction of the results of this demonstration? Provide reason for your prediction.
2. Which substance was a better conductor of heat?
3. What type of heat transfer was involved?

MOVING WATER

1. What is your prediction of the results of this demonstration? Provide reason for your prediction.
2. Record the results for each set of bottles.
3. What type of heat transfer was involved?

THE HEAT RACE

1. What is your prediction of the results of this demonstration? Provide reason for your prediction.
2. Record the results. Give at least one explanation for these results.
3. What type of heat transfer was involved?

THE CANDLE SNUFFER

1. What is your prediction of the results of this demonstration? Provide reason for your prediction.
2. Record the results. Why does this happen?
3. What type of heat transfer was involved?

RISING AND SINKING COLUMNS

1. What is your prediction of the results of this demonstration? Provide reason for your prediction.
2. Record the results. Why does this happen?
3. Would you always expect this result? Why?

HOT AIR BALLOON

1. What is your prediction of the results of this demonstration? Provide reason for your prediction.
2. Record the results. Why does this happen?
3. What happens to the molecules of a substance when it heats?

Conductometer

1. What is your prediction of the results of this demonstration? Provide reason for your prediction.
2. Record the results. How did the results compare with your predictions?
3. List the metals in order from the best conductor to the worst conductor.
4. What type of heat transfer was involved?

Blended Water

1. What is your prediction of the results of this demonstration? Provide reason for your prediction.
2. Record the results. How did the results compare with your predictions?
3. List the metals in order from the best conductor to the worst conductor.
4. What type of heat transfer was involved?

Lesson 13

THAT LITTLE CUPCAKE HAS HOW MANY CALORIES?

Subjects and Skills	Science, Language Arts, Mathematics
Rationale	This activity allows students to investigate the real-world concept of calories, as well as why different foods seem to give you more energy than others.
Objectives	The students will be able to (1) build a calorimeter, (2) use data collected from the calorimeter to calculate the amount of calories and kilocalories in a peanut and marshmallow, and (3) make predictions between their data and other food choices.

Activity Preparation

1. To save time, you can have the coat hanger calorimeters already bent, as well as pieces of aluminum foil already cut and ready to be placed on the calorimeter.
2. Briefly discuss Calories (1 Calorie = 1000 calories) and the difference between Calories and calories.

Activity Procedures

1. Set up the calorimeters by bending the coat hangers so they will stand on their own with the hook of the hanger bent over the opening created by bending the hanger (see Figure 3 for complete set up).
2. Completely cover the outside of the calorimeter (hanger) with aluminum foil to focus all the heat forward toward the hanger hook.
3. Bend the tab of the aluminum can up (the can will hang by this), and fill the can with 10 mL of water. Hang the can on the hook of the coat hanger.
4. Using the clay, make a small ball, and place the head of the long pin in the ball of clay.
5. Place this ball on the foil under the can. There should be enough clearance that when the peanut or marshmallow is placed on the pin, it does not touch the can.
6. Record the temperature of the water in the can.

Figure 3. Calorimeter set-up.

7. Place the peanut or marshmallow on the pin and light it on fire.
8. When it has completely burned out, record the new temperature of the water in the can.
9. Dispose of the burnt item, refill the can with 10mL of tap water and record its temperature.
10. Place the other item on the pin and allow it to burn. Record the new temperature after the item has completely burned out.

Note: Although this experiment is set up with just peanuts and marshmallows, my students enjoyed bringing other foods in to test; other proteins (nuts, pepperoni), and sugars such as cereals and snack cakes burned quite well, and students created another column in their data table for their brought object. In the post-lab questions, they also processed how their food compared to the marshmallow and peanut results.

Materials Needed (per group)

Aluminum foil
Clay
Graduated cylinder
Long pin
Matches
Mini marshmallow
Nutritional information for both peanuts and marshmallows
Peanut (fresh in shell works well)
Soda can
Thermometer
Water
Wire coat hanger

The Calorimeter Lab

PROBLEM

Which food provides more energy for the human body: peanuts or marshmallows?

PRE-LAB QUESTIONS

1. Define Calorie and calorie.

_____

_____

_____

2. How are Calories related the energy found in food?

_____

_____

_____

DATA COLLECTION

	Peanut Values	Marshmallow Values
Amount of water used	mL	mL
Grams of water used (1 mL = 1 g)	g	g
Temperature of water before burning the food item	°C	°C
Temperature of water after burning the food item	°C	°C
Temperature change	°C	°C
Number of calories produced in burning of the food item	c	c
Number of Calories in the food	C	C

Name: _____ Date: _____

1. Which food item had more calories? Examine the nutritional information for that food. How close were your calculations to the actual measures printed? Why do you think this is?

_____

_____

_____

_____

2. What ingredients do you think your food items contain that could explain your results?

_____

_____

_____

_____

3. Compare your results to those of other groups. How similar were your results? Give two reasons why their results may have been different than your own.

_____

_____

_____

_____

4. If you were preparing for an athletic event, which item would be a better choice to eat? Explain your choice.

_____

_____

_____

_____

Lesson 14

WHAT MAKES A SCIENTIST FAMOUS? PRESENTATIONS

Subjects and Skills	Science, Oral Presentation Skills, Technology
Rationale	This activity allows students the opportunity to research and present relevant information and provide positive and constructive feedback for their peers.
Objectives	Students will (1) prepare an oral presentation to accompany a PowerPoint presentation about a famous scientist and (2) as an audience member, provide positive feedback to fellow presenters.

Activity Preparation

1. Discuss the three criteria for the presentation (content, correctness, and prop; see p. 41 for details).
2. Distribute feedback forms and review how to give positive feedback and the characteristics of a good audience.
3. Discuss how transition time will be handled to be the most effective.

Activity Procedures

1. Each student will need to present his or her timed PowerPoint presentation. Although there is not a required minimum time for the presentations, in order to present all of their information, most presentations will be approximately 3–5 minutes, with only about 2 minutes transition time. For an average class size of 25 students, teachers should plan to devote 2–3 days for these presentations.
2. Each student should complete a feedback form after the conclusion of each presentation.
3. After the presentation is complete, the presenter can walk around, collect the feedback forms and submit them to the teacher. While the feedback forms are being collected, the next presenter should be loading his or her presentation.
4. The teacher can take a quick look at the feedback forms for appropriate comments. The teacher may also choose to allow some of the presentation points to be determined by an average of the numbers submitted by the audience.
5. Rubrics and feedback forms can be returned once the grade has been recorded.

Materials Needed

Presentation Feedback Forms (see p. 64; enough for each student to provide feedback for each presenter)

Presentation Feedback Form

Topic: _____   Presenter's Name: _____

On a scale of 1–10, rate the following areas.

Content (How well did the speaker know the information? Did the information appear to be correct? Was he or she able to answer questions?)		Please provide one short reason why you gave this number.
Flow (Did the presentation flow smoothly? Was the speaker confident and ready to speak?)		Please provide one short reason why you gave this number.
Prop (Did he or she explain why he or she chose the prop? Did the choice seem logical? Do you think it was the best choice?)		Please provide one short reason why you gave this number.

Topic: _____   Presenter's Name: _____

On a scale of 1–10, rate the following areas.

Content (How well did the speaker know the information? Did the information appear to be correct? Was he or she able to answer questions?)		Please provide one short reason why you gave this number.
Flow (Did the presentation flow smoothly? Was the speaker confident and ready to speak?)		Please provide one short reason why you gave this number.
Prop (Did he or she explain why he or she chose the prop? Did the choice seem logical? Do you think it was the best choice?)		Please provide one short reason why you gave this number.

Chapter 5

States of Matter and the Fluid Laws

States of Matter Overview

The states of matter, as well as properties of fluids, are the building blocks for chemistry and physics, because all matter exists in one state or another. Most students have a lot of background knowledge in the three states of matter and can provide multiple examples of solids, liquids, and gasses without any difficulty. This unit delves further into the properties and unique qualities of each state of matter, as well as phase changes that take place. It exposes students to the properties of one of the most interesting solids (dry ice), and allows students to investigate the phase change of water, as well as various unexpected results caused by the fluid laws. This unit often is tied into many of the other units depending on the curriculum developed by each school district. It may be part of an introduction to chemistry, a study of physical and chemical changes, or an energy or heat unit. Therefore, this is a shorter unit meant to be supplemental to other units.

Objectives for States of Matter

By completing the lessons in this chapter, the students will be able to:
- identify the four states of matter;
- express properties of the different states of matter;
- explain the processes that take place during phase changes;
- create a phase change graph; and
- understand and identify examples of the fluid laws, including Boyles' Law, Charles' Law, Pascal's Principle, Archimedes' Law, and Bernoulli's Principle.

Chapter Activities

Below is an outline of the lessons included in this chapter. Depending on the prior knowledge of your students, you can pick which activities you want to use to reinforce the concepts.

In Lesson 15, students will see how the states of matter change by making ice cream in zipper bags. It can be completed and eaten within one 55-minute class period. This experience usually has a component in which the students get to enjoy the ice cream after creating it. If your school has a policy about the use of food in the classroom, be sure and obtain permission from your administration.

Lesson 16 exposes the students to the simple concept of moving water through its three phases and recording the temperature at which each phase changes. By going through this experience, and measuring the temperatures on their own, students realize that boiling can begin before 100°C and that the temperature does not change significantly during the phase change.

Dry ice (solid CO_2) is a substance everyone enjoys because of its property of sublimation. Dry ice is made by compressing liquid carbon dioxide into a block form. Its uses range from cold food storage to removing dents from cars. Lesson 17 presents six small activities to help students explore dry ice. However, keep in mind that there are certain safety considerations (it is possible to get a burn from a cold object) when working with dry ice.

Lesson 18 introduces students to some of the fluid laws and principles by using key words and associations. Although they may seem like advanced concepts, students really enjoy being able to use these laws to explain observations around them (as well as in the rotational labs in Lesson 19).

Supplies and managing equipment can be a problem in the science classroom. By setting up a rotational lab like the one in Lesson 19, students can have access to materials and equipment, but the teacher only needs one set of equipment. These rotational labs are card based—all of the instructions can be copied onto cards and laminated for durability. These experiences are shorter and exploratory in nature.

Vocabulary for
This Chapter

Archimedes' principle: the Greek mathematician Archimedes stated that the buoyant force on an object in a fluid is equal to the weight of the fluid displaced by the object

Bernoulli's principle: the Swiss scientist Daniel Bernoulli stated that as the velocity of a fluid increases, the pressure exerted by the fluid decreases

boiling point: the temperature at which a liquid becomes a gas

Boyle's law: British scientist Robert Boyle stated that the volume of a gas decreases when the pressure increases, provided the temperature stays the same

Charles' law: French Scientist Jacques Charles stated that the volume of a gas increases when temperature increases, provided the pressure stays the same

condensation: the change of a substance from a gas to a liquid, which usually takes place when a gas is cooler or below its boiling point

evaporation: the gradual change of a substance from a liquid to a gas at temperature below the boiling point

fluid: any material that flows; liquids and gases are fluids

freezing point: the temperature at which a liquid becomes a solid

gas: the state of matter without definite shape or volume

liquid: the state of matter defined by a definite volume, but no definite shape

melting point: the temperature at which a solid becomes a liquid

Pascal's principle: French Scientist Blaise Pascal stated that pressure applied to the fluid is transmitted without change through the fluid

solid: the state of matter defined by a definite volume and shape

sublimation: the process in which a solid changes directly to a vapor without forming a liquid

Lesson 15

I Scream, You Scream!

Subjects and Skills	Science, Language Arts, Mathematics
Rationale	This activity allows the students to experience a real-world phase change.
Objectives	Students will (1) review the states of matter and (2) identify components that are needed for a phase change to take place.

Activity Preparation

1. Gather the ingredients for the ice cream, making sure to put the cold items in a school refrigerator and freezer until you are ready to use them.
2. Review the concepts of states of matter and freezing point with your students.

Activity Procedures

Note: This activity will produce a little more than ½ cup of ice cream per bag. Depending on the number of students and supply availability, each student can create their own bag, or it can be completed in groups.

1. Pour 240 mL of milk into the quart-sized zipper bag.
2. Dissolve the 10 grams of sugar into the milk.
3. Add 2 mL of vanilla to the mixture; close the bag securely and shake to mix.
4. Place the quart bag in a gallon-sized zipper bag.
5. Fill larger bag with ice cubes and add 20 grams of rock salt. Close the larger bag securely.
6. Gently, but continually, massage or shake the bags together to keep the contents of the inner bag mixing. You do not want the inner bag to open!
7. After about 15–20 minutes the mixture should be solidified into ice cream.
8. Open the larger bag. Dispose of its contents in the garbage can after removing the inner bag. Rinse off the outside of the inner bag. If the group is sharing the ice cream, open the inner bag and distribute the ice cream into cups and enjoy.
9. Have students answer the post-lab questions in their lab notebooks, or on a separate piece of paper.

Materials Needed (per group)

Ice cubes
8-ounce cups (if groups are sharing the ice cream)
240 mL milk (approximately 1 cup)
20 grams rock salt
10 grams sugar
2 mL vanilla
Zip-closing gallon-sized bag
Zip-closing quart-sized bag

1. What phase changes took place in this experiment? Think of all of the ingredients, as well as any other phase changes based on your observations.
2. Assuming that your larger bag did not leak, why did the outside become wet?
3. Why must you continuously mix the milk mixture?
4. Why did you need to add salt to the ice?
5. How does this experiment relate to the real world?

Lesson 16

I'm Melting

Subjects and Skills	Science, Mathematics, Language Arts
Rationale	This experiment exposes students to the mathematics behind an everyday phase change.
Objectives	The students will (1) make and record observations as water changes its phase, (2) create a phase change diagram for water, and (3) identify the relationship between phase change and energy.

Activity Preparation

1. Review safety considerations when using hotplates or heat sources.
2. Discuss what happens to the particles in a substance as heat or energy is added and the phase begins to change.
3. Have students record their prediction of at what temperature (in Celsius) all of the ice will be melted, as well as at what temperature gas bubbles will begin forming, on a separate sheet of paper.

Activity Procedures

1. Divide students into groups, giving each a copy of the I'm Melting Experiment (pp. 70–71).
2. Have students follow the procedure as listed.
3. Students will use notebook paper to record their hypothesis, data, graph, and post-lab questions.

Materials Needed (per group)

Hot plate (or heat source)
Ice
Beaker (or heat resistant container for heating ice)
Thermometer
Graph paper

I'm Melting Experiment

PURPOSE

To observe the temperature and phase changes of a substance as it is heated.

HYPOTHESIS

Record your prediction of at what temperature (in Celsius) all of your ice will be melted, as well as at what temperature gas bubbles will begin forming (meaning the water is boiling).

PROCEDURE

1. Fill the beaker half full of tightly packed ice. Place the thermometer into the center of the ice; be sure it is not resting on the bottom of the beaker.
2. Take your initial reading of the temperature at 0 seconds for your data table.
3. Place the beaker on the hot plate, and adjust for medium heat.
4. Immediately begin to measure the temperature of the ice.
5. Measure and record the temperature of the ice every 30 seconds and record it in your data table below. Record the percentage of each phase inside the beaker. For example, you could record 10% liquid, 90% solid.
6. When the water is boiling and the temperature has remained the same for at least 3 minutes (usually about 20–25 minutes after beginning the experiment), you may end the lab. Turn the hot plate off, remove the thermometer, and allow the water to cool before removing it from the hot plate and disposing of it. Graph your data and answer the analysis questions.

DATA

Create the following data table on your own paper to record the temperatures from Step 5.

Phase Change Lab Data Table		
Time (Minutes)	Temperature (°C)	Phase(s) Present / Observations
0		
0.5		
1		
1.5		
Continue table to –		
24.5		
25		

Name: _____ Date: _____

Using graph paper, graph your data. On your graph, label the following: solid phase, liquid phase, gas phase, melting point, boiling point.

POST-LAB QUESTIONS

Answer the following questions on a separate piece of paper.

1. What phases did you observe?

2. What two phase changes did you observe during this lab?

3. As the ice was melting, heat was added to it. Did the temperature increase during melting? Why or why not?

4. What was happening to the ice or water when the line on the graph was horizontal?

Lesson 17

Subjects and Skills	Science, Language Arts, Mathematics
Rationale	This experiment will expose students to a real-world example of sublimation, as well as the unique physical properties of dry ice (carbon dioxide gas in solid form.)
Objectives	Students will (1) investigate and (2) observe the properties of dry ice.

Activity Preparation

1. Review the How Can Dry Ice Be Dry? Investigation Sheet (pp. 74–75) to familiarize yourself with the activities the students will be conducting.
2. Dry ice now can be purchased at most grocery stores. Be sure you have a cooler ready so that you keep the majority of the dry ice intact.
3. Using a hammer, carefully break the dry ice into smaller manageable pieces before the experiment.

Activity Procedures

1. Have students create their own lab sheet by folding a piece of lined paper into sixes, giving them six sections on the front of the paper.
2. Have students number each section 1–6. Each number represents one of the dry ice experiences. Students will record the information for each numbered lab in its appropriate square.
3. Before beginning their experiment, students can then set up each square of their lab paper to record their predictions (hypothesis), observations, and questions.
4. Reinforce safety concerns when using dry ice. Students will use only one piece of dry ice for this lab. Because dry ice can cause burns, students should not handle it with bare hands. Students also should use safety goggles to protect against flying objects.
5. Students should briefly discuss the pre-lab discussion questions in their groups and record their responses on the back of their lab paper.
6. As a whole group, have students share their answers and add additional information to their papers as needed so their responses are complete.
7. Briefly explain each mini-lab and its expectations to students. Students can make any specific notes on safety on their lab paper for each station.
8. After completing the six experiences, student should complete the post-lab discussion question on the back of their lab paper.

Materials Needed (per group)

Beaker/plastic cup
Birthday candle
Clay
Clear film canisters
Dry ice

Forceps or tongs
Graduated cylinder
Hammer
Masking tape
Matches
Meter stick
Plastic wrap
Thermometer
How Can Ice Be Dry? Investigation Sheet (p. 74)

How Can Ice Be Dry? Investigation Sheet

ACTIVITY 1: DESCRIBING DRY ICE

1. Place a piece of dry ice on the lab table.
2. Record all the physical properties of dry ice, including the states of matter that are present.
3. Compare and contrast dry ice and ice created from water.

ACTIVITY 2: SUBLIMATION

1. Using forceps or tongs, place the dry ice into a plastic beaker or clear cup.
2. Place a piece of plastic wrap over the mouth of the cup and securely seal the cup.
3. Record your observations. Explain what is causing what you observe.

ACTIVITY 3: WHAT IS THAT GAS?

1. Place the birthday candle in a small lump of clay.
2. Light the candle.
3. Using the sealed cup from Activity 2, carefully remove one corner of the plastic wrap and "pour the gas" out of the cup over the flame. Do not let the piece of dry ice fall onto the candle.
4. Record your observations. How are your observations related to density? Based on your observations, how might this property of dry ice be used in the real world?

ACTIVITY 4: FAST CHANGE

1. Create a data table to record temperature changes.
2. Measure 20 ml of water and record its temperature.
3. Add the water to the remaining sample of dry ice from Activity 3.
4. Keeping the thermometer in the water, not touching the dry ice, record the temperature changes every 10 seconds until the temperature becomes constant.
5. What did you observe as the temperature changed? What patterns did you notice as the temperature changed?
6. Explain what causes the sounds that you hear as the temperature changes.

ACTIVITY 5: ICE PUCKS

1. Using a meter stick, create a start and finish line by placing two pieces of tape 20 cm apart.
2. Place a small piece of dry ice in front of the start line.
3. Using a pencil, slide the block of ice across the tabletop trying to come to rest as close to the finish line as possible.
4. Record your observations. What allows the dry ice to move in this manner?

ACTIVITY 6: DRY ICE ROCKETS

1. Place a small piece of dry ice into the film canister.
2. Optional: Add 2–3 ml of water.
3. Place the cap on the film canister, turn it upside down and place it cap down on the table and wait.
4. Record your observations. Using scientific vocabulary, explain what caused this to happen.
5. Dry ice is one type of solid propellant. Name two other solid propellants that are commonly used and their purpose.

POST-LAB DISCUSSION

Is dry ice appropriately named? Write a paragraph to defend your response with your observations of the experiments conducted today.

_____

_____

_____

_____

_____

_____

_____

_____

_____

_____

_____

_____

_____

_____

_____

_____

Lesson 18

Subjects and Skills	Science, Art
Rationale	This activity will allow students to make creative connections in order to remember abstract concepts.
Objectives	The students will be able to express properties of fluids, as well as key examples of Boyles' Law, Charles' Law, Archimedes' Principle, Bernoulli's Principle, and Pascal's Principle.
Activity Preparation	1. Students will need to prepare their windowpane by folding their white paper to create six equal rectangles.
Activity Procedures	1. Discuss each of the fluid laws with students. Specific examples are included on the Teacher's Guide to the Fluid Fellows (p. 77). 2. After discussing the specific examples, students can create a picture in each windowpane to represent each fluid law. 3. Under each picture, students should write the law in their own words.
Materials Needed	White paper Teacher's Guide to the Fluid Fellows (p. 77)

Teacher's Guide to the Fluid Fellows

Boyle's Law: "Bouncing Baby Bawls Because Balloon Breaks"	Have students imagine they have given a balloon to a baby. If the baby were to grab that balloon and squeeze it really quickly, what could happen? (It breaks.) What would cause this to happen? (The pressure increases.) When the baby squeezes the balloon, what happens to the volume of the balloon? (It decreases.) Therefore, as volume decreases, pressure increases (or conversely, as volume increases, pressure decreases).
Charles' Law: "Crazy Charlie in the Hot Air Balloon"	Have students picture a wacky scientist having a really hard time with the hot air balloon he is trying to inflate. Will a fan be enough to inflate a hot air balloon? (No, you need heat.) As you apply heat to the air inside the balloon, what happens inside the balloon? (It inflates.) So, what relationship can be draw between volume and hot temperatures? (As temperature goes up, volume goes up.) This is Charles' Law—as temperature increases, volume increases (or conversely, as temperature decreases, volume decreases).
Pascal's Principle: "Paste Pressing Preferences"	Ask students: If you have a brand-new tube of toothpaste, is one method more effective than another for getting the paste out of the tube? Why can you press anywhere and the paste will still come out the open end? (No matter where you press, the particles push each other—like dominoes—until the paste finds its way out.) This is Pascal's Principle—pressure will be transferred equally through a fluid. Pascal's Principle also takes into consideration the amount of pressure that is transferred. If you karate-chop the middle of the toothpaste, does it still come out slowly? Pascal's Principle states that pressure will be transferred equally throughout a fluid—no matter your paste-pressing preference.
Archimedes' Principle: "The Large Greek Going Down With the Ship"	Share a picture of Archimedes with students and tell them the following story of Archimedes and his "eureka" moment: King Hieron had commissioned a local goldsmith to make his crown. The king, however, was worried that the goldsmith had cheated him by adding some other metals to the crown and keeping the extra gold for himself. The king asked Archimedes to determine if the crown was solid gold. The challenge Archimedes faced was that he could not do anything to do the crown to determine its composition. Normally he would have melted the crown and formed it into a cube to determine its density. Puzzled by the problem, Archimedes went to take his bath. As he got into the bath, he noticed that the water level changed as he got in. After seeing this he realized that he could use this method to determine the volume of the crown. It did not have to be in a cube shape. He could then calculate the density of the crown. He was so excited, he ran through the streets naked, crying "Eureka!" Archimedes' principle? The object immersed in a fluid is buoyed up by a force equal to the weight of the dispersed fluid. Once students have pictured this, ask them to think of Archimedes on the Titanic sitting comfortably on one of the lounge chairs on the deck, enjoying the sunset. Unfortunately, when the ship strikes the iceberg, even Archimedes' principle could not save the Titanic. Why not?
Bernoulli's Principle: "Bad, Bad Shower Curtain"	Ask students if they ever have to fight the shower curtain's attraction to their body after turning on the water. Do particles move to areas of higher pressure (lots of particles bumping each others) or lower pressure (not as many particles)? As water leaves the showerhead, it begins to push the air in front of it in the same direction that the water is traveling. As the air travels quickly past the shower curtain (and this effect is intensified when the bather is closer to the curtain), it creates an area of low pressure, which affects the lightweight shower curtain. Fighting the shower curtain is an example of Bernoulli's law, which states that if you increase the velocity of a fluid, it will create an area of lower pressure.

Lesson 19

FLOWING FLUIDS ROTATIONAL LAB

Subjects and Skills	Science, Language Arts, Mathematics
Rationale	This activity allows students to experience different examples of physics concepts and explain observations by applying their knowledge.
Objectives	Students will be able to (1) make predictions based on prior knowledge, (2) record accurate observations, and (3) using their knowledge of gas laws, explain observations made in the rotational labs.

Activity Preparation

1. Prepare for the Cartesian Catsup activity by testing the packets in a glass of water. The packets without enough air will sink; those with too much air will lie on top of the water. You want one that floats vertically near the top of the glass. Fill a clear 2-liter bottle with water. Place your chosen catsup packet in the bottle. Replace the bottle cap. Squeeze the bottle to be sure the catsup packet rises and lowers smoothly.

2. Gather the materials for each of the rotational lab. Set up a station for each lab, or buckets with all the supplies that can be taken to student desks.

Activity Procedures

1. Have students create their own lab sheet by folding a piece of lined paper into fours. Have them number each square with 1–8. Each number represents one of the rotational labs.

2. Before beginning, students can set up each square of their lab paper with places to record their predictions (hypothesis), observations and questions, and the law or principle being demonstrated by the specific station.

Suggestions and Expectations for the Flowing Fluids Mini-Labs

Here are some suggestions and expectations for a few of the labs.

Station 1: The Old Water in the Cup Trick: The students will be able to remove their hand from the card and it will remain seemingly "stuck" to the cup because the air pressure presses the card to the cup.

Station 2: The Can Can (Charles' Law): To allow this station to move a little faster, have one can heating at the beginning of class, so the first group that comes will set up a can for the next group and use the one that was already hot. Demonstrate how to move the can in one smooth movement quickly from the hot plate to the ice bath. Students often are apprehensive of the results and do not move quickly, making the result not as dramatic.

Station 3: A Sweet Treat (Boyle's Law): As students decrease the pressure in the syringe by pulling out the plunger, the marshmallow will grow in volume. As they increase the pressure by pushing in the plunger, the volume will decrease.

Station 4: Cartesian Catsup (Pascal's Principle and Boyle's Principle): As students press on the bottle, the pressure transfers equally throughout the fluid, creating pressure in the catsup packet. As the pressure increases, the volume of air inside the packet decreases, so that it can no longer float and will begin to sink.

Station 5: Can You Move? (Bernoulli's Principle): As students blow through the center of the cans, they create an area of low pressure. The cans will move into this area.

Station 6: Ping-Pong Moves (Bernoulli's Principle): As the water flows over the ball, it speeds up, creating an area of low pressure. Although it seems like the ball would move away from the water, it actually is drawn into the lower pressure area.

Station 7: Get a Closer Look! (Bernoulli's Principle): As students blow across the top of the straw, they speed up the pocket of air, creating an area of low pressure. The water from the cup will move up the straw into the area of low pressure and create a spray of water. Have students get really close to observe this.

Station 8: Cold Hands, Warm Air? (Charles' Law): Place at least eight or nine bottles in one ice bath at one time so there is always a really cold one waiting for the group. As the student's hands warm the bottle, the temperature inside the bottle also is warmed, causing the volume to expand. Students can expect to see the warmer air bubbling in the bottle.

....

Materials Needed
(for 7 groups)

2-liter plastic bottle
Nine aluminum soda cans
Beaker or cup
Beaker tongs
5–10 catsup packets
Two clear plastic syringe (30CC or larger; without needles)
Clear straws (one approximately 6 cm in length, plus one for each student)
Food coloring
Graduated cylinder
Hairdryer
Hot plate
Two ice baths
21 index cards (must be larger than the mouth of the cup)
14 mini-marshmallows
Ping-pong ball
Two rigid plastic bottles (baby bottles work well for this)
Plastic container (large enough to submerge rigid plastic bottle)
Plastic container for ice
Plastic cup

Materials: Plastic cup, water, index card (larger than the mouth of the cup), plastic container

Procedure:
1. Fill the plastic cup with water, leaving about 1 centimeter of air in the cup.
2. Place an index card over the mouth of the cup.
3. Predict what will happen when you invert or flip the cup upside down and remove your hand. Record your prediction.
4. Be sure your hand is dry! Holding the cup and card over the plastic tub, put your hand on top of the card and invert the cup, holding the card in place.
5. Take your hand away from the card slowly.
6. Record your observations.

Questions:
1. Using scientific vocabulary, explain why this happens.
2. Record the law or principle at work.

STATION 2: THE CAN CAN

Materials: Hot plate, aluminum soda can, water, pan with ice, beaker tongs, graduated cylinder

Procedure:
1. Place 5 ml of water in the soda can.
2. Place it on the hot plate; this will be for the next group.
3. You will be using the can that is now producing steam.
4. Make a prediction about what will happen when the can is flipped into the ice bath.
5. Using the beaker tongs, quickly flip the can upside into the ice bath (so the opening goes down into the ice—this way no gas escapes!)
6. Record your observations.

Questions:
1. Why did this happen?
2. How does temperature affect particle movement?
3. Record the law or principle at work in this experience.

STATION 3: A SWEET TREAT

Materials: Mini-marshmallows, two clear plastic syringes

Procedure:
1. Using your lab paper, record your predictions for the two following situations: the pulling of the plunger and the pushing of the plunger.
2. Place the marshmallow in the large syringe. Cover the end of the syringe.
3. Pull out the plunger.
4. Record your observations.
5. Release the plunger and remove your finger from the end.
6. Dispose of the marshmallow.
7. Place a new marshmallow in the syringe.
8. Pull the plunger all the way out, and cover the end of the syringe with your finger.
9. Push in the plunger.
10. Record your observations.
11. Throw away the marshmallow.

Questions:
1. What happens to the volume of air as you pulled the plunger out? Pushed it in?
2. Would any food work for this experience? Why or why not?
3. Record the law or principle at work.

STATION 4: CARTESIAN CATSUP

Materials: Cartesian Catsup Bottle

Procedure:
1. What do you think will happen when you squeeze the bottle?
2. Gently squeeze the bottle.
3. Record your observations.

Questions:
1. Does the force you use to squeeze the bottle make a difference in your observations? Explain.
2. What is happening inside the catsup packet when you squeeze the bottle?
3. Why is it moving as it does?
4. Record the law or principle at work.

STATION 5: CAN YOU MOVE?

Materials: Two aluminum soda cans, straw

Procedure:
1. Lay the two cans on their sides approximately 5 cm apart (so they can roll).
2. After reading the next step, record your prediction for this station.
3. Using your straw to focus the airflow, blow between the two cans. Try not to specifically blow the cans, simply between them.
4. Record your observations.

Questions:
1. By blowing between the two cans, explain what is happening to the air molecules as you do this.
2. Would this experiment work if the cans were upright? Why or why not?
3. Record which law or principle is at work.

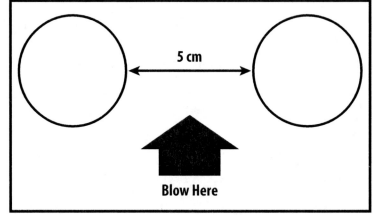

5 cm

Blow Here

STATION 6: PING-PONG MOVES

Materials: Hairdryer, ping-pong ball

Procedure:
1. After reading the procedure below, make a prediction of what you will observe.
2. Turn on the hairdryer and place the ping-pong ball in the airflow.
3. Try different angles of airflow, as well as different heights for placing the ball in the airflow.
4. Record your observations.

Questions:
1. How did the angle of the airflow affect the ping-pong ball?
2. What seemed to determine where the ping-pong ball would stay in the airflow?
3. What keeps the ping-pong ball in its location?
4. Draw a diagram that shows how the air moves in this experiment.
5. Record which law or principle is at work.

STATION 7: GET A CLOSER LOOK!

Materials: Beaker (or clear cup), colored water, clear straw (approximately 6 cm), students' straws

Procedure:
1. After reading the procedure, record your predictions.
2. Place the clear straw into the colored water.
3. Move close enough to watch the colored water in the clear straw.
4. Using your straw, blow a strong blast of air across the top of the clear straw. (Do not blow into the clear straw, simply across the top.) See the graphic provided.
5. Record your observations.

Questions:
1. Why is colored water used for this experiment?
2. Using scientific vocabulary, explain why this happened.
3. Record the law or principle that is at work.

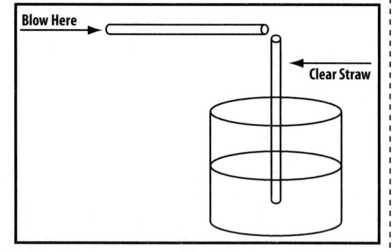

STATION 8: COLD HANDS, WARM AIR?

Materials: Two rigid plastic bottles, ice bath, plastic container with water

Procedure:
1. Predict what will happen when a cool bottle is submerged in water.
2. Remove one of the empty bottles from the ice bath.
3. Submerge the bottle in the water, try not to tip the bottle or allow water into the bottle.
4. Wrap your hands around the bottle and observe.
5. Record your observations.
6. Place your bottle back into the ice bath.

Questions:
1. What did the cool empty bottle contain?
2. Explain what caused your observations.
3. Would this have worked without your hands being wrapped around the bottle? Why or why not?
4. Record the law or principle for this experience.

Chapter 6

Simple Machines

Throughout this unit, students will analyze the six different kinds of simple machines in greater depth. This will include the three classes of levers, wheel and axles, pulleys, inclined planes, wedges, and screws. Humans use simple machines on a daily basis to complete everyday crucial tasks, from eating (lifting food to our mouths with our arms: a lever, chewing the food: a wedge and lever), to moving (legs and ankles are levers, too). This unit opens students' eyes to all of the simple machines around them and their impact and importance in their daily lives.

Depending on the prior experiences of the students, they may have some knowledge of the different types of simple machines, but usually they do not. This unit allows them to investigate and explore the different types first on a basic level through a window paning activity before moving to their complexities in a categorization quiz. By the end of the unit, students will understand that simple machines impact their daily lives and that most simple machines they use actually are more complex than simple.

This unit is centered on one of the most popular and long-awaited projects of the physics units—the mousetrap car. Students will apply all of their knowledge of simple machines in the building, showing, and racing of a mousetrap car using recycled and reused materials. Once the cars are built, students also will have the opportunity to examine the cars of their peers and provide positive feedback on the various cars they examine. This feedback is often valued even more than the teacher's!

By completing the lessons in this chapter, the students will be able to:
- identity and provide examples of the different types of simple machines,
- classify simple machines into categories,
- discuss the impact and importance of simple machines in our daily lives, and
- build an example of a simple machine.

Below is an outline of the lessons included in this chapter. Depending on the prior knowledge of your students, you can pick which activities you want to use to reinforce the concepts. I suggest that you start with the project introduction so that all of the information and concepts presented during the class will tie back into the project.

Lesson 20 is a favorite among the students. When asked each year to choose their most favorite project, the mousetrap car always receives more than half the votes. Allow at least 3 weeks for students to complete the project. Lesson 21 is introductory in nature. After discussing or taking notes on the different types of simple machines, students are ready to apply the information and draw key examples of the different types of simple machines. The categorization quiz in Lesson 22 presents pictures of various simple machines and their classifications. Students classify the machines and then work as a group to produce one common answer document. This really encourages discussion and understanding of the different types of machines.

After studying all of the different simple machines in depth, Lesson 23 allows students to evaluate their importance and significance. Students will create a flapbook and prioritize the different types of simple machines in order of importance to the human race, as well as the impact on the world if each type of simple machine ceased to exist.

Lesson 24 is an experimental design activity that allows students to investigate levers in a new and exciting way. This activity poses the question—using only certain materials, how could you create a simple machine that can shoot a marshmallow one meter? Students then design a machine and experiment with various designs in order to answer the question.

Students really enjoy participating in the car show of Lesson 25. They bring their car for show, set up their area, and then rotate around the room commenting on everyone else's car. Students really enjoy reading the comments of their peers. The next day will be the races when students demonstrate that their car can "go the distance."

Vocabulary for This Chapter

axle: the pin, bar, or shaft on which or by means of which a wheel rotates

effort arm: the part of a lever on which an effort force is applied

fulcrum: the fixed point around which a level pivots

inclined plane: a sloping surface (ramp) used to raise objects

input force: the force applied to a machine in order for work to be done, also called the effort force

lever: a bar that is free to pivot (rotate) around a fixed point (fulcrum)

mechanical advantage: the number of times a machine multiples the effort force applied to it

output force: the force exerted by a machine in order for work to be done, also called the resistance force

pulley: a simple machine consisting of a grooved wheel with a rope or chain running along the groove.

resistance arm: the part of a lever that exerts the resistance force

screw: a special type of inclined plane wrapped in a spiral around a cylindrical post

wedge: a moving inclined plane with one or two sloping sides, such as knives and chisels

wheel and axle: two different sized wheels that rotate together, such as a doorknob

Lesson 20

MOUSETRAP CAR PROJECT INTRODUCTION

Subjects and Skills   Science

Rationale   This project encourages students to show their creativity, create an original design to meet certain criteria, and test their designs.

Objectives   The students will (1) develop a design for a mousetrap car that will travel at least 2 meters given design criteria, and (2) construct their mousetrap car.

Activity Preparation   Although not necessary, it does help if there are a few examples of both good and bad mousetraps cars for the students to examine. These should be removed after a few days, so students do not try to reproduce the examples. There are many pictures of mousetrap cars available online, as well books detailed in the Resources section of this book. A basic labeled diagram (see Figure 4) has been included for the teacher's use. It is very important that students understand that there are various other options and methods of creating mousetrap cars that still meet the rubric's criteria; the included diagram is just a very basic mousetrap car.

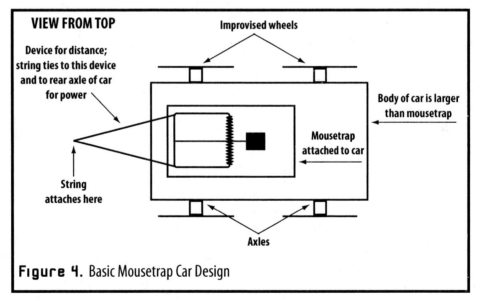

Figure 4. Basic Mousetrap Car Design

Activity Procedures

1. Give each student a copy of the Mousetrap Car Project Rubric (p. 89).
2. Discuss the grading with students. The project is worth up to 200 points, rather than the usual 100 points, although the grade can still be recorded as a percentage.

3. Discuss each grading criterion with the students, providing examples and explanations for each. Encourage students to give examples of each to clarify their knowledge. One criterion to enforce is that students do not use rat traps—these traps can break fingers. Reiterate that cars must be made of recycled materials.

4. This discussion usually takes about 45–50 minutes. After the discussion, students are now ready to proceed on their own, brainstorming their ideas, and beginning the design process.

Materials Needed   Mousetrap Car Rubric (p. 89)

Name: _____ Date: _____

Mousetrap Car Project Rubric

Criteria	Excellent	Good	Fair	Poor
Mousetraps Used	15 *points* Used more than one mousetrap; traps work effectively.	10 *points* Used one mousetrap; trap works effectively.	5 *points* Used one mousetrap; trap does not work.	0 *points* Used a rat trap.
Car Parts Car cannot use manufac-tured parts.	10 *points* All parts are recycled.	6 *points* 90% of the parts are clearly recycled.	4 *points* 50% of the parts are recycled.	0 *points* More than 50% of the parts are store bought.
Wheels Must be improvised (e.g., spools, CDs).	10 *points* Wheels obviously are recycled, improvised, and creative.	6 *points* One set of wheels is recy-cled and improvised; other is not.		0 *points* Wheels are store bought or originally intended for a car.
Body Shape Is Extended Beyond Mousetrap	10 *points* Body shape is extended beyond mousetrap.			0 *points* Body is mousetrap.
Axles	10 *points* Both sets of wheels have axles.	6 *points* One set of wheels has an axle.		0 *points* Wheels do not have axles.
Originality Car is unique to owner in design and use of materials.	15 *points* Unique design and use of materials.	10 *points* Unique use of materials; design is not unique.	5 *points* Design is unique; materials are not.	0 *points* Neither design nor materi-als are unique
Decoration Does not include original decoration on materials used.	10 *points* Car is painted or covered and decorated.	6 *points* Car is just painted or covered.	4 *points* Car has minimal painting, covering, and decoration.	0 *points* No painting, covering, and decoration.
Traction	10 *points* Traction on all four wheels.	6 *points* Traction on one set of wheels.		0 *points* No traction.
Device for Distance Includes a rod or U attached to mousetrap.	10 *points* Rod or U is present.			0 *points* Device is not present.
Distance Traveled	85 *points* Car moves 2 meters on the ground.	50 *points* Car moves 1 meter.	10+ *points* 1 point added for each 2 centimeters traveled up to 1 meter.	0 *points* Car does not move.
Rubric	10 *points* Student returns rubric.			0 *points* Rubric is not returned.
$1 Rule Student does not spend more than $1 on car, includ-ing the trap. Can spend more than $1 to purchase and use additional traps.	5 *points* Can prove he or she did not spend more than $1, or he or she did spend more than $1, but purchased and used additional traps.			0 *points* Cannot prove he or she did not spend more than $1.

Total Grade: _____
(Out of 200)

Lesson 21

SHOW ME THE MACHINE!

Subjects and Skills	Science, Art
Rationale	This activity allows students to create and draw their own examples of each type of simple machine.
Objectives	Students will (1) decide on a representational example of each type of simple machine and (2) create a meaningful drawing of each example.
Activity Preparation	1. Prepare the information you would like to share with students about simple machines.
Activity Procedures	1. Have students fold their paper in fours.
	2. Discuss each type of simple machine, including the three types of levers.
	3. Have students label each box with a type of simple machine.
	4. Students should decide on the best example for each simple machine and draw a picture to represent each simple machine.
	5. Students should label any key parts of the simple machines:
	• Levers should have fulcrums, resistance arm, and effort arms labeled.
	• Wheel and axle should have both the wheel and axle labeled.
Materials Needed	Lined paper

Lesson 22

SIMPLE MACHINES AREN'T SO SIMPLE

Subjects and Skills Science

Rationale This activity has students looking at everyday objects and their functions from many different perspectives and sharing their thoughts and ideas with peers.

Objectives The students will be able to (1) classify the different types of simple machines and (2) defend their classifications.

Activity Preparation
1. This activity works best using pictures displayed on a large screen. Photo clip art or digital pictures taken of the various objects can be used as examples.
2. Obtain pictures of the items listed on the answer key on p. 92.

Activity Procedures
1. Students need to set up their paper for the quiz by folding their paper once lengthwise and then into four squares, so that there are eight total squares. Label each square with the types of simple machines: first class levers, second class levers, third class levers, wheels and axles, pulleys, inclined planes, wedges, and screws.
2. Explain that they will be shown various pictures of simple machines. Most of the machines will fit into more than one category; for example, anything that is a wedge also is an inclined plane. Each picture should stay up for about 20 seconds.
3. After a picture is shown, give the name of the object students are to record, as well as how many boxes in which its name should be recorded. It is helpful to start out by using a laser pointer to point out the different parts that make a simple machine more than one type. For example, when looking at a picture of a knife, using the laser pointer, point to the sharp edge of the knife and say "this is one simple machine (wedge/inclined plane), the other simple machine is how you use it (second class lever)."
4. Once the students have recorded all of their answers, explain that this is actually a group quiz. Each group now has exactly 10 minutes to discuss, debate, check, and decide upon all of the correct answers.
5. Each group will need to submit everyone's papers stapled together; the top paper is the one that will be graded for the group.

Materials Needed Pictures or images of simple machines
Simple Machine Categorization Quiz Answer Key (p. 92)

Simple Machine Categorization Quiz Key

Item Name	Number of Boxes	Types of Simple Machines
Axe	3	wedge, inclined plane, third or first class lever (varying)
Baseball bat	1	third class lever
Bicycle tire	1	wheel and axle
Bolt	2	screw, inclined plane
Can opener	3	inclined plane, wedge, wheel and axle
C-clamp	3	inclined plane, screw, wheel and axle
Crane	1	pulley
Door knob	1	wheel and axle
Door stop	2	inclined plane, wedge
Drill bit	3	inclined plane, wedge, screw
Egg beater (handheld)	4	inclined plane, wedge, screw, wheel and axle
Electric fan	3	inclined plane, wedge, wheel and axle
Flagpole	1	pulley
Hammer	3	inclined plane, wedge, third or first class lever (varying)
Jar lid	2	inclined plane, screw
Knife	3	inclined plane, wedge, second class lever
Ladder	1	inclined plane
Nail	2	inclined plane, wedge
Needle	3	inclined plane, wedge, first class lever
Pencil sharpener	4	inclined plane, screw, wedge, wheel and axle
Rake	3	inclined plane, wedge, third class lever
Ramp	1	inclined plane
Roller blade	1	wheel and axle
Sailboat	4	pulley, inclined plane, wedge, wheel and axle
Scissors	3	inclined plane, wedge, first class lever
Screw	2	inclined plane, screw
Screwdriver	3	inclined plane, wedge, wheel and axle
Seesaw	1	first class lever
Stairs	1	inclined plane
Stapler	3	inclined plane, wedge, second class lever
Wheelbarrow	2	second class lever, wheel and axle
Wishing well	1	pulley

Lesson 23

MACHINES MAKE HISTORY

Subjects and Skills	Science, Language Arts
Rationale	This activity allows students to ponder and theorize how our world and its history are impacted by simple machines.
Objectives	The students will (1) prioritize the simple machines in order of their impact on humanity, and (2) defend their choices by choosing examples of the impact of various simple machines on our daily lives.
Activity Preparation	1. It is best to have one flipbook already folded as an example.
	2. Review the types and various examples of simple machines.
	3. Brainstorm the impact of simple machines on the daily lives of students.

Activity Procedures

1. Students need to fold their papers to create a flipbook with 10 flaps (see Figure 5), stapling across the top fold.

2. Students will list the eight simple machines in order from least important to most important considering their use to humans, their historical significance, and how the world would be different if they had never existed.

3. Each student should record the simple machines in order on the flaps. He or she should place the most important machine on the largest (bottom) flap to allow the greatest amount of space for expressing his or her ideas.

Figure 5. Simple Machine Flap Book Setup

4. As they open the flaps, students will draw pictures of significant examples of each simple machine to illustrate their choice of order.

5. On the back of the bottom flap, students will write a paragraph to defend their choice of order. This paragraph should address all of the aspects they took into consideration to make their decision.

Materials Needed (per student)	4 pieces of legal size white paper
	1 piece of legal size colored paper (used for cover page)

Lesson 24

THE CATASTROPHIC CATAPULT LAB

Subjects and Skills	Science, Language Arts, Math
Rationale	This activity presents students with a problem and allows them to develop a plan to solve the problem and test and modify their ideas.
Objectives	Students will (1) create plans for an effective catapult that will launch a marshmallow one meter and (2) test and modify their catapult plans.

Activity Preparation

1. Review examples of first class levers, including identifying the effort (input) arm, fulcrum, and output (resistance) arm.

Activity Procedures

1. Reinforce that this experiment has many possible results and the goal is for their group to use certain materials to meet certain guidelines. Everyone's experiment will be different.
2. Introduce the problem: How can we use these materials to create a machine that can launch a marshmallow at least one meter?
3. Although this may seem very general, this experience is meant to be investigative and based on trial and error. Students may ask for more clarification and instruction. If this happens, encourage the students to think of all of the possibilities that these general guidelines will allow them.
4. Allow time for students to design and plan their catapult and record their procedure for building their design on their lab sheet. Their procedure should include measurements and be specific enough that if the procedures were given to other students, they could reproduce the intended catapult.
5. When the planning stage is over, allow time for the building of the catapult and finally the testing with the marshmallow.
6. Once a successful catapult has been developed, have the students make a drawing of their final catapult on their lab report, labeling the effort arm, resistance arm, and fulcrum, as well as record their responses to the post-lab discussion questions.

Materials Needed (per group)

Two rubber bands (provide a choice of many sizes)
Scissors
15 straws
Large marshmallow
Styrofoam cup
Styrofoam plate
45 cm tape
Two toothpicks

Catastrophic Catapult Lab

PURPOSE

In this experiment, you will be working with variations of the lever, a simple machine. By experimenting and manipulating its design, your group will be trying to create a device that can launch a marshmallow at least 1 meter.

BASIC CONSTRUCTION GUIDELINES FOR YOUR CATASTROPHIC CATAPULT

You have access to all the materials below but *do not* have to use them all in your design.

Materials Available:
- Two rubber bands (your choice of sizes)
- Scissors
- 15 straws
- Styrofoam cup
- Styrofoam plate
- 45 cm tape
- Two toothpicks

CONSTRUCTION PLANS/BRAINSTORMING

Use this space to record or brainstorm construction ideas for your Catastrophic Catapult.

Name: _____ Date: _____

Once you have developed a successful catapult, record your building procedures here. Remember to be very specific about the steps you take to construct your Catastrophic Catapult. Use enough detail and measurements that someone else could recreate your catapult.

_____

_____

_____

_____

_____

_____

Below, draw your successful catapult. Label the effort arm, resistance arm, and fulcrum.

POST-LAB DISCUSSION QUESTIONS

1. What class of lever is your catapult? How do you know this?

_____

_____

_____

2. How would you have to alter your catapult if you were trying to launch a heavier object, say a small rock?

_____

_____

_____

Lesson 25

CAR SHOW AND OFF TO THE RACES!

Subjects and Skills	Science, Mathematics
Rationale	This activity allows students to provide positive feedback for their peers and showcase their own product.
Objectives	Students will (1) critique classmates' mousetrap cars on three different criteria, (2) provide positive feedback for other mousetrap cars, and (3) demonstrate the distance their car can travel.

Activity Preparation

1. A few days before the car show, assign each student a number for his or her car. This will be his or her "racing number." It should be permanently displayed on his or her car.
2. *Optional*: Send home invitations for the parents to attend the car show and car races. Parents really enjoy coming to see the ideas of other students, and students enjoy showing their cars to other adults.
3. The race course will need to be marked using chalk or masking tape. It works best if each meter is marked with a line and its measurement. To accommodate the record-breaking cars, at least 25 meters should be marked.

Activity Procedures

1. On the first day of the car show, distribute the Mousetrap Car Evaluation Sheet (pp. 99–100).
2. Students should fill in their car's name, as well as their own. This paper will stay beside their car as their classmates rotate from desk to desk, writing comments about the cars.
3. Before beginning the rotations, discuss each criterion that students will be evaluating: creativity of design, creativity of decoration, and use of materials. Students will be rating cars on a scale of 1–10. A perfect score is a 10, while a 1 would be used for someone who did not meet the project requirements.
4. The last column is available for specific and positive feedback for the car. It is expected that each student will make a positive comment for each car. "Great!" is not specific enough, instead, students might comment with "Great theme, I like soccer too!"
5. Have each student rate his or her own car on the first line of the evaluation sheet. The students will rotate from car to car in an orderly manner. They should only need about 2 minutes at each car. Simply calling "Switch" is an effective way to keep everyone on track.

6. On day 2, the race day, in order to keep students actively involved, have them create a data table for predicting the distance each car will go when raced and what feature of each car leads them to make that prediction.

7. As students get ready to race, they should hold up their cars, tell their car number, and allow students to predict the distance their car will travel. As students are holding up their cars for predictions, two more students should be winding their cars, so there always is a car ready to race.

8. Once predictions are made, cars should be placed behind the starting line, and allowed to run. The distance recorded is where the back wheels stop.

9. It is customary to allow the option for two runs in case the car turns or does not work well the first time; however, if the car travels more than 3 meters, the student sometimes will choose not to rerun the car. If they do wish to race again, they will become one of the winders while the next student races.

10. Once all of the cars have been raced, students can begin working on the questions on the back of the Mousetrap Car Evaluation Sheet.

Materials Needed   Masking tape or chalk
Meter stick
Mousetrap Car Evaluation Sheet (pp. 99–100)

Name: _____ Date: _____

Mousetrap Car Evaluation Sheet

Your Number	Creativity of Design (1–10)	Creativity of Decoration (1–10)	Use of Materials (1–10)	Comments

Name: _____ Date: _____

Mousetrap Car Evaluation Sheet, Continued

Car's Name _____

Answer each question in paragraph form.

Did you enjoy this project? _____ Explain why you enjoyed it or not.

What did you find most difficult about this project? Why?

What was the easiest part of the project? Why?

If you could do your project over again what would you do differently? Why?

Chapter 7

Static and Current Electricity

Static and Current Electricity Overview

Electricity, be it current electricity (electricity in motion) or static electricity (electricity that builds up on an object and is suddenly released), is around us everyday. We depend on current electricity to light our homes and provide energy to the starters in our cars so they can be used. Although we do not depend as heavily on static electricity, it does exists around us from those shocking carpet experiences, to lightning strikes.

Most students have been exposed to examples of both types of electricity, and have usually experimented with creating a basic circuit using a light bulb, wire and battery. Although this unit does begin at this level by having students create a basic circuit, it also asks them to look at circuits from new perspectives to really understand the components of a closed circuit. In addition to the details of the circuit, students also investigate how energy is produced and used in the home. This unit centers on a multiphase energy conservation project that students will conduct in their homes. This project walks students through all of the steps of the scientific process. Students research energy conservation, evaluate the research for its effectiveness in their own situation, make a plan, put it into effect for 2 weeks, gather data, and evaluate their plan.

Objectives for Static and Current Electricity

By completing the lessons in this chapter, the students will be able to:
- create simple series and parallel circuits,
- predict whether a material is a electrical conductor or insulator based on its properties,
- develop a plan for energy conservation and test its effectiveness,
- express how they can impact energy usage in their daily lives, and
- state various ways to conserve electricity in their homes.

Chapter Activities

Below is an outline of the lessons included in this chapter. Depending on the prior knowledge of your students, you can pick which activities you want to use to reinforce the concepts. I suggest that you start with the project introduction so that all of the information and concepts presented during the class will tie back into the project.

Lesson 26's Energy Conservation Project asks students to develop a plan for conserving electricity in their home. By following all of the steps of the scientific method, they will put their plan into effect and evaluate their efforts. Lesson 27 has students investigate five different questions regarding how energy is used in the home in order to help them better understand how to conserve energy. Once students have researched how energy is used in the home, they will develop a chart of ideas for conserving energy in Lesson 28. Each idea will be evaluated for its feasibility and application in their situation.

Based on the ideas from the feasibility chart, students will develop a specific list of ideas that they can do at home in order to try and conserve electricity in Lesson 29. In order for students to gather data each day during their project, they will need to know how to read the electricity meter, as well as how to write journal entries that explain the significance or changes in the data. Lesson 30 teaches these skills to students.

The investigational lab in Lesson 31 is introductory in nature. It allows students to explore the various ways to create a simple circuit using a battery, light bulb, and wires. Once students have created simple circuits, these simple circuits can be used in Lesson 32 to test various everyday household substances to discover if they are electrical conductors or insulators.

After experiencing simple parallel and series circuits, it often is difficult to effectively create complex circuits without having a lot of materials. Lesson 33 presents various complex challenges to students. Students will be asked to become a part of the circuit and create specific circuit situations with multiple correct answers.

Vocabulary for This Chapter

circuit: a closed path through which electrons (electricity) flow

closed circuit: a circuit that does not have any breaks or openings

conductor: a material that resists or blows the flow of electrons

dry cell: a power source that acts as an electron pump and generates electric current by chemical reaction; "dry" because it uses a thick, pasty electrolyte

feasible: capable of being done or accomplished

insulator: a material that resists or blows the flow of electrons

kilowatt: a unit of power; equal to 1000 watts (W)

kilowatt hour (kWh): the unit of electrical energy; 1 kilowatt-hour (kWh) = 1000 watts (w) of power used for 1 hour

open circuit: a circuit that has a break or opening that stops the flow of electrons

parallel circuit: an electrical circuit where the current flows through more than one path; if one path is interrupted, current will still flow through the other paths

resistor: a material, substance, or object that uses energy by slowing down the flow of electrons as they pass through it

semiconductor: an element that conducts electricity under certain conditions

series circuit: a circuit with only one path for electrons

switch: a device for turning on or off or directing an electric current or for making or breaking a circuit

Lesson 26

CAN ONE PERSON HAVE AN IMPACT? ENERGY CONSERVATION PROJECT

Subjects and Skills   Science, Language Arts, Research Skills, Mathematics

Rationale   This activity illustrates the scientific method by allowing students to develop a product that progresses through all of the processes and allows students to see that they can have an impact on the world around them by making small changes.

Objectives   Students will (1) research ways to conserve energy, (2) evaluate the feasibility of various methods of conservation, (3) develop a conservation plan, (4) execute an energy conservation plan in their home, (5) record data on electricity usage for 2 weeks, and (6) evaluate and suggest improvements to an electricity saving plan.

Activity Preparation   1. Students will need to obtain information about the average amount of kilowatt-hours used in their household during various time periods during the year. This information may take a little time to acquire and can be obtained from the electricity company. This project usually takes at least 4 weeks from start to finish, which generally is enough time as long as the students request this information immediately. Note: Acquiring this information can sometimes be a sensitive subject with parents, especially because the information often is accompanied by the amount paid. Therefore, it is often best to leave how this information is acquired up to each family. Once parents understand why it is needed, they usually are very willing to assist in obtaining the information.

Activity Procedures   1. Discuss the idea of conservation of electricity by asking the following questions:
   a. What are some of the different ways to produce electricity?
   b. How is energy produced locally? Is it deregulated, and what does that mean?
   c. What are the personal and global benefits of conserving electricity?
   d. Are there drawbacks to conserving energy?

   2. Give each student a copy of the Energy Conservation Project Rubric (p. 104). This project is different in that students will not be ready to start on the project immediately; parts of the rubric should be explained as students complete the various steps and are ready to progress.
   3. Discuss the overall plan or global aspect of this project: Developing an energy conservation plan for their home and testing it.
   4. The project is worth up to 220 points, rather than the usual 100 points, although the grade can still be recorded as a percentage.

Materials Needed   Electricity Conservation Project Rubric (p. 104)
The Electricity Conservation Project Guidelines (pp. 105–106)

Static and Current Electricity

Energy Conservation Project Rubric

Criteria	Excellent	Good	Fair	Poor
Research Questions Includes questions and answers; must be typed; includes bibliography.	30 *points* All questions are present and completed with answers; all typed; includes accurate bibliography.	20 *points* All questions presented, but not all completely answered, handwritten, or bibliography is inaccurate.	10 *points* All questions presented but some are left blank, or no bibliography is present.	0 *points* Questions are not present.
30 Ideas/Hypothesis Includes chart of 30 ideas to conserve electricity; students must explain why or why not the idea will conserve electricity and how it will do so.	30 *points* Includes chart of 30 ideas to conserve electricity; all have explanations; feasibility is addressed on each.	20 *points* Includes chart of 30 ideas; only half have explanations or feasibility missing.	10 *points* Chart has less than 30 ideas or more than half of the ideas have no explanation or feasibility.	0 *points* Chart not present.
Contract/Procedure Completed and signed by due date; included in binder.	25 *points* Contract completed and signed; choice for plan is well-thought-out and feasible.	15 *points* Contract completed and signed; choice for plan is not the best, but conducted well.	5 *points* Contract completed and signed; choice for plan is present, but purpose is unclear/unfeasible.	0 *points* No contract or no plan of action included.
Preliminary Data Kilowatt-hours (kWh) used daily during the week before the experiment.	10 *points* Kilowatt-hours used daily during the week before the experiment is accurately recorded in data table.			0 *points* Kilowatt-hours are not recorded.
Actual Data Kilowatt-hours used daily during the contract time.	20 *points* Kilowatt-hours used daily during the contract time is accurately recorded in the data table and graphed.		5 *points* Data table is complete, graph is not present or incorrect.	0 *points* Data table and graph are not present.
Journal Includes meter reading, kWh used, and 4–5 sentence explanation of why that amount was used.	20 *points* Includes meter reading, kWh used, and 4–5 sentence specific and significant explanation of why that amount was used for each day of the contract period.	10 *points* Missed more than 2 days of journaling or 1–3 entries have less than 4–5 sentence explanations.	5 *points* Missed 3 or more days of journaling, more than 3 days have less than 4–5 sentences, or all readings are present, but do not have explanations.	0 *points* Journal is not present.
Reflections Reflections include both questions and answers written in paragraph form; answers are well-thought-out.	15 *points* All reflection questions and answers are present, completed in correct form, and well-thought-out.	10 *points* Reflection questions are all present, some answers are incomplete; most answers are well-thought-out.	5 *points* Not all reflection questions are present or answers are very brief and not well-thought-out.	0 *points* Reflections are not present.
Conclusion Complete paragraph describing what the student did, learned, and what he or she will continue doing.	15 *points* Describes what the student did, learned, and what he or she will continue doing in paragraph form.		5 *points* Paragraph only describes what student did or learned.	0 *points* Paragraph not present.
Parent Statement	45 *points* Includes two things he or she observed student doing; handwritten and signed.		10 *points* Typed with signature or does not mention specific things the student did.	0 *points* Statement not present.
Rubric	10 *points* Turned in with project.			0 *points* Rubric not returned.

Total Grade: _____

(Out of 220)

Name: _____ Date: _____

The Energy Conservation Project Guidelines

You will complete the following steps in your energy conservation project. Keep your records for each step neatly and in order in a folder or binder, with each step clearly labeled.

STEP 1: RESEARCH QUESTIONS

Must include both question and answer, typed.

1. Explain in a paragraph why it is important to conserve energy. Be sure to include facts from your research.
2. What household items use the most energy? (List at least five.) For each item, think about how it works and explain why it might use a lot of energy.
3. For each of the items listed in Question 2, list three ways you could cut back on their energy use in your home.
4. Inventory your home (ask your parents if you are not sure) and list all of the major appliances that use gas instead of electricity.
5. Think about the various conditions that occurred last year around this time. Write a paragraph explaining what you think used most of the electricity in your home during that time period and why.
6. List your research sources using proper bibliographical form.

STEP 2: FEASIBILITY CHART

Must contain 30 items with appropriate explanations about why the idea would work in your home or not.

STEP 3: CONTRACT

Must have your parent's signature and must contain at least 15 items from your list of 30.

STEP 4: EVALUATION

Your evaluation of your project should include the following:
- Kilowatts used the *week* before the experiment (including a data table and readings).
- Kilowatts used *daily* during contract period (include data table of usage and graph).
- *Diary*: 4-5 daily sentences that includes your meter reading, the kWh used, as well as an explanation about why you believe the number changed as it did. This is specific to the project (not who likes who, or who gave you a note today). *Example:* Today we used 45 kWh, all because of my brother's birthday party. I kept telling the children to turn out the lights, but they wouldn't listen. They played video games for hours. Considering we had about 16 six-year-olds, I suppose it wasn't as bad as it could have been.
- *Reflection Questions* (all answered in paragraph form):
    1. Did you follow your contract? How well?
    2. Of the 15 strategies you chose for your contract, what did you find easiest to do? Why?

3. Of the 15 strategies you chose for your contract, what did you find most difficult? Why?

4. Do you feel you did everything you could have to make your project successful? Explain.

5. If you could do this project again, what strategies would you repeat? What would you change? Explain your answers.

6. Would you classify your project as successful? Why or why not?

- *Conclusion*: Write a paragraph that explains what you learned from the project, and why it is a good example of the scientific process.

STEP 5: PARENT STATEMENT

- This statement must be handwritten (in your parent's handwriting, not yours with their signature). This must include at least two things they saw you do during the experimentation period.

- This does not have to be anything formal. It can be as simple as two to three sentences stating specific actions you have taken during your experiment.

Lesson 27

PART 1 OF PROJECT: MY AQUARIUM USES HOW MUCH ELECTRICITY?

Subjects and Skills	Science, Language Arts, Research Skills
Rationale	This activity has students completing the first and most often skipped step of the scientific process: research.
Objectives	Students will be able to (1) identify ways to conserve energy in the home and (2) state why conserving energy is important.
Activity Preparation	1. Internet and computer access is vital to the success of this project. If a teacher does not have access to a computer lab, various pages from helpful Web sites can be printed as resources for students to use in their research. 2. Prepare a list of Web sites that will be beneficial for students to use. It is usually good idea to begin with your local electric company's Web site.
Activity Procedures	1. Students are ready to begin the first part of the project—the research. 2. Using the various Internet resources, students should investigate the research questions and take notes in order to gather information on each question. 3. Once they have enough information for a complete answer, students can compose paragraph responses for each of the questions.
Materials Needed	Research Questions (p. 108) Various Web sites and resources

Research Questions

Answer the following questions on your own piece(s) of paper.

1. Explain in a paragraph why it is important to conserve energy. Be sure to include facts from your research.

2. What household items use the most energy? (List at least five.) For each item, think about how it works and explain why it might use a lot of energy.

3. For each of the items listed in Question 2, list three ways you could cut back on their energy use in your home.

4. Inventory your home (ask your parents if you are not sure) and list below all of the major appliances that use gas instead of electricity (if any).

5. Think about the various conditions that occurred last year around this time. Write a paragraph explaining what you think used most of the electricity in your home during that time period and why.

6. List your sources using proper bibliographical format.

Lesson 28

PART 2 OF PROJECT: I THINK I CAN, I THINK I CAN!

Subjects and Skills	Science, Language Arts
Rationale	This activity allows students to brainstorm ideas to conserve energy, both reasonable and creative, and evaluate and defend their ideas.
Objectives	Students will (1) use research to develop a list of ways to conserve electricity in the home and (2) evaluate the feasibility of using these methods to conserve electricity.
Activity Preparation	1. Review that the purpose of brainstorming is to list as many ideas as possible to answer a question or solve a problem.
Activity Procedures	1. Once the research questions are answered, students are ready to begin part two of the project—making a feasibility table for their conservation ideas. This chart will list at least 30 different ideas for conserving energy in the home. Students should not worry about whether their ideas are feasible at this time.
	2. Students then should evaluate each idea for its feasibility in their home, and provide an explanation for why they made this evaluation. Ideas should not be determined to be feasible or unfeasible until the students have discussed them with their parents, as their parents may be already considering some of the students' ideas and be open to the change.
Materials Needed	Computer access

Lesson 29

PART 3 OF PROJECT: SIGNING ON THE DOTTED LINE

Subjects and Skills   Science, Language Arts

Rationale   This activity allows students to take ownership of their specifically designed experiment.

Objectives   Students will (1) design a contract or plan for conserving electricity in their own home, and (2) share their energy conservation ideas with their family.

Activity Preparation

1. Students will need to review the components of a complete contract:
   - date the contract is initiated is recorded,
   - parties impacted by the contract are identified,
   - initiatives being put into action during contract are clearly stated, and
   - signature of all parties involved in the contract are obtained.

Activity Procedures

1. Discuss how to state specific measurable energy conservation statements. The statements should be written in such a way that anyone could confirm that it took place. Rather than saying they will use TV less, students could say, "I will turn off the TV every time I leave the room and not leave it on to fall asleep." This is a statement that can be evaluated each day.
2. Using their feasibility charts, students should focus on the ideas they thought would be most feasible and develop a list of at least 15 specific and measurable ideas that they will put into place for their experiment.
3. Students should share their preliminary contracts with the teacher to be sure the conservation statements are well stated and specific.
4. Contracts then can be taken home to share with family members. Although students usually will want everyone in the family to sign the contract, at least one parent or guardian should sign the contract so he or she is aware of what the student is trying to accomplish. The entire family does not have to be involved in the contract's goals; however, greater results are seen when everyone participates. There still will be recognizable changes if only the student follows the contract.

Lesson 30

LOOK AT ALL OF THOSE DIALS

Subjects and Skills	Science, Language Arts, Mathematics
Rationale	This activity empowers students by providing them with specific information necessary to record data effectively.
Objectives	Students will learn how to (1) read the dials of an electric meter in order to record daily data for their project and (2) write effective journal entries to explain the data they observe.
Activity Preparation	1. Prepare an overhead of the Student Meter Reading Activity Sheet (p. 112).
Activity Procedures	1. Although some meters have digital readings, the majority of them still show kilowatts using a set of four or five dials. If students have a meter with only four dials, the last number is recorded as a zero to provide a 5-digit number.
	2. Walk students through the first meter reading on the sheet.
	3. The first dial moves clockwise, so students will record the number it is has just passed. In the sample this would be 6.
	4. The second dial moves counterclockwise; students again will record the number it has just passed, or 0.
	5. The third dial moves clockwise, so it would be 2.
	6. The fourth dial moves counterclockwise so it would be 8 (although it is close to 9, it has not passed it yet).
	7. The last dial moves clockwise and would be 3.
	8. For the reading, simply record the numbers in order: 60283
	9. Students can then work on Part 2 on their own. They should record meter readings and kilowatts used daily and then write a 4–5 sentence summary of what could have happened in the home to match these results. Perhaps there was a party, they were traveling, or it was an average day for the family.
	10. Students should be creative, yet realistic in their journal entries.
	11. This activity mirrors the data collection and journal entries that are required for the project, so students can use this as a reference when it is time to record their information.
Materials Needed	Meter reading sheet

Student Meter Reading Lesson Sheet

PART 1: READING AN ELECTRIC METER

Reading electric meters may look quite complicated, but it is actually quite easy once you realize how the dials are set up. Below you will see a figure that shows the arrangement of a typical electric meter. You will notice that the dials have the numbers 0–9, but some of them are arranged clockwise while others are counterclockwise.

Recognizing which way the dial moves is the secret to accurately reading your electric meter. Looking at the above meter, record the readings for each dial below:

_____ _____ _____ _____ _____

  first dial   second dial   third dial   fourth dial   fifth dial

This will be the initial reading.

The next day, if the meter is read 24 hours later, it reads: 60302. How many kilowatts were used in the 24-hour period? _____ Is this a reasonable number? _____ How do you know?

_____

_____

_____

_____

_____

_____

PART 2: READING THE METER AND RECORDING JOURNAL ENTRIES

The following meters represent a week of meter readings. Although it is not a real house, the numbers are realistic. For each day, record the meter reading, calculate the kilowatt usage, and then create a journal entry that could match the data. The first day is the initial reading, and should state the reading and what the recorder hopes to accomplish during their week of reading the meter.

Monday:

Reading: _____
Journal entry for the day:

_____

_____

_____

_____

Tuesday:

Reading: _____ Kilowatts used since yesterday _____
Journal entry for the day:

_____

_____

_____

_____

Wednesday:

Reading: _____ Kilowatts used since yesterday _____
Journal entry for the day:

_____

_____

_____

_____

Thursday:

Reading: _____ Kilowatts used since yesterday _____
Journal entry for the day:

_____

_____

_____

_____

Name: _____ Date: _____

Friday:

Reading: _____ Kilowatts used since yesterday _____

Journal entry for the day:

_____

_____

_____

_____

Write a paragraph summarizing the data you gathered. How did this family do monitoring their electricity usage? Did they seem to be successful? Use data from the electric meter readings to support your opinions.

_____

_____

_____

_____

_____

_____

_____

_____

_____

_____

_____

_____

_____

_____

Lesson 31

LIGHT UP MY LIFE LAB

Subjects and Skills	Science, Language Arts
Rationale	This activity allows students to use the trial and error technique to facilitate experimentation.
Objectives	Students will (1) design various configurations of wire, batteries, and light bulbs to create closed circuits and (2) determine the components necessary to create a closed circuit.
Activity Preparation	1. Assemble experiment kits containing one battery, two pieces of wire, and a miniature light bulb.
	2. Prepare additional wires with stripped ends to have on hand, as the bare ends do break with use.
	3. Take this opportunity to review the basic structure of the light bulb including the filament and how it produces light through heat. The way in which batteries produce power also can be reviewed at this time if needed.
Activity Procedures	1. Propose the experimental problem: "Can you devise five or more ways to make a light bulb light up using only one battery and two pieces of wire?"
	2. Before distributing the experiment kits, ask the groups to draw at least five different configurations to test as their hypothesis.
	3. Once groups have made at least five different predictions, distribute the experiment kits.
	4. Students should test their ideas, as well as experiment with other ideas. All of the ideas they try should be drawn and recorded on their lab report. Each idea also should be recorded as successful or unsuccessful.
	5. Process the experiment by discussing the post-lab questions, or if using a formal lab report, students can answer the post-lab questions as part of their conclusion.
Materials Needed (per group)	Battery Miniature light bulb Two pieces of plastic coated wire with the ends stripped (5–8 cm in length) One pair of wire cutters for the teacher Light Up My Life Lab (p. 117)

Light Up My Life Lab

PROBLEM

What are at least five different ways to light up a light bulb using only one battery and two pieces of wire?

HYPOTHESIS

Draw pictures to show your predictions in the box below.

DATA

Draw all of the different combinations of circuits you tried. Be sure and label each one as successful or unsuccessful.

Name: _____ Date: _____

1. What is the difference between an open and closed circuit?

_____

_____

_____

_____

_____

_____

2. What are the necessary components for a closed circuit?

_____

_____

_____

_____

_____

_____

3. How might adding batteries or light bulbs impact a circuit?

_____

_____

_____

_____

_____

_____

Lesson 32

COMMON CONDUCTORS AND INTERESTING INSULATORS

Subjects and Skills	Science, Language Arts
Rationale	This activity allows students to develop their own experimental testing method and test their ideas about the properties of electrical insulators and conductors.
Objectives	Students will (1) develop an experiment to classify objects as electrical conductors and insulators, and (2) identify characteristics of electrical insulators and conductors.

Activity Preparation

1. Prepare bags of the materials that will be tested, as well as those needed to create a basic circuit.

Activity Procedures

1. Introduce the problem: How could a simple circuit be used to identify electrical insulators and conductors?
2. Share the materials that each group will have available for building the "tester," as well as the predetermined objects they will need to test. They should choose at least five additional objects that they would like to test.
3. After brainstorming their ideas, students should make a drawing that illustrates their final design. Students need to create a data table for recording the predictions for each object, as well as the results of the testing of each product.
4. Discuss or record responses to the post-lab discussion questions below.

Materials Needed (per group)

Paper clip
Pencil
Penny
Ruler
String
Tape
Other objects that students choose to test

Post-Lab Discussion Questions

1. What seems to be the common properties of good conductors? Name three substances that you did not test that you believe would be good conductors.
2. What are properties that good insulators have in common? Name three substances that you did not test that you believe would be good insulators. Name a specific situation where having an electrical insulator would be helpful.
3. Based on the name *semiconductors*, what results do you think could be observed in this experiment if they were tested? Record an example of a semiconductor. How are they used?

Lesson 33

Subjects and Skills	Science
Rationale	This activity encourages students to look at complex situations in a concrete way and solve problems cooperatively with their peers.
Objectives	Students will (1) work cooperatively to (2) draw complex circuit diagrams that meet given criteria.

Activity Preparation

1. Create a set of large circuit cards for each group. See Figure 6 for small examples of the cards.

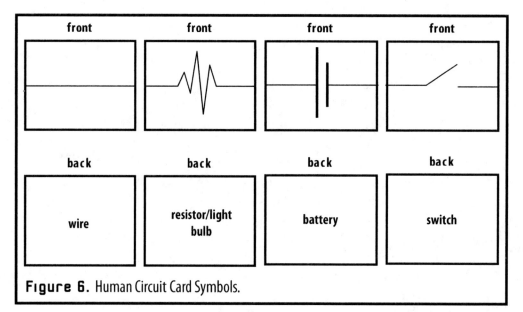

Figure 6. Human Circuit Card Symbols.

2. Copy each type of card onto a different color paper, making it easier for students to find the cards they are looking for. Laminate the cards for durability.
3. This activity will be a culmination of the information on circuits presented during previous instruction. Therefore, students will need to review the components of a complete circuit, open and closed circuits, and the paths that electrons take in series and parallel circuits and their impact on the resistors.

Activity Procedures

1. Discuss the use of symbols in order to make complex drawings easier to understand.
2. Introduce the four symbols that students will be using in their circuit building. The circuit cards should have symbols on one side and the words on the other.

3. Break students into groups of 4–5 and give each group enough desk or floor space to spread their circuit cards out in front of them.

4. Give each group the circuit problems to work on. They become progressively more difficult.

5. As they tackle the problems, some students will prefer to use the symbol side of the cards, others will prefer the words.

6. Wander around and answer questions as students create their various circuits.

7. Most groups will ask the teacher to check their circuits as they are developed.

Materials Needed (per group)
Six dry cell (battery) cards
Eight resistor cards
Eight switch cards
25 wire cards
Be the Electron! Problems (p. 122)

Be the Electron! Problems

PROBLEM #1

Create a circuit that has four light bulbs and four dry cells. When you turn on the switch, two light bulbs turn off, and the other two stay on.

PROBLEM #2

Create a circuit that has three dry cells and three resistors, so that when the switch is off, one of the resistors is off.

PROBLEM #3

Create a circuit that has eight dry cells, six resistors, and two switches, so that when one switch is off, all of the resistors are off (like a circuit breaker) and when the other switch is off, three resistors are on and three resistors are off.

PROBLEM #4

Create a circuit that has four dry cells and seven resistors. It should be set up in such a way that with three resistors, if one resistor burns out, they all turn off (they are controlled by one switch). The other resistors are set up so that if one is turned off, the others stay on. There also is a breaker switch that controls the entire circuit.

PROBLEM #5: CHALLENGE PROBLEM

Create a circuit with one resistor and a switch next to the battery so that when the switch is *on*, the light bulb is off.

Chapter 8

Magnetism

Magnetism Overview

Magnetism is a concept that is integrated into other units depending on curricular expectations. The most popular placement for this information is with electricity, although it can also be included into chemistry in the discussion of physical properties. It has been separated into this small unit so that it can be placed appropriately based on curricular demands. No matter its placement, magnetism is a concept with which most students are very familiar. From refrigerator magnets to compasses, most students have been exposed to magnetism. They naturally are curious about why magnets will "stick" to certain items. Students usually can state whether a magnet will be attracted to a certain object or not, simply because they have tested them at home. This unit takes students from this point and allows them to investigate the properties of magnetism, the presence of magnetic insulators and conductors, and using electricity to produce a magnetic field.

Objectives for Magnetism

By completing the lessons in this chapter, the students will be able to:
- explain the property of magnetism,
- discuss the variables that impact the strength of an electromagnet, and
- identify properties of magnetic conductors and insulators.

Chapter Activities

Below is an outline of the lessons included in this chapter. This chapter is not centered on a product; instead it is introductory and exploratory in nature. Teachers could choose which activities they would like to use to supplement their current lessons.

After discussing the aspects of magnetism, Lesson 34 asks students to make connections between the concepts by using web cards. Students will have the opportunity to discuss and share their ideas as they manipulate the concept-based cards.

The experimental design experience in Lesson 35 provides the students the materials they need to create a simple electromagnet. Once created, they can test the variables that impact the strength of electromagnets.

Students usually are familiar with electrical conductors and insulators, but what about magnetic conductors and insulators? Lesson 36 asks students to test various substances to discover which are magnetic conductors and insulators, as well as identify their common properties.

Vocabulary for This Chapter

conductor: a material that allows or strengthens magnetic fields

electromagnet: strong temporary magnet made by inserting an iron core into a wire coil and passing an electric current through the coil

insulator: a material that blocks magnetic fields

magnetic field: the region around a magnet where magnetic forces act

magnetic pole: the ends of a piece of magnetic material where the magnetic forces are strongest, labeled north pole (N) and south pole (S)

magnet: a piece of iron or of certain other materials that attracts or repels other pieces of iron

Lesson 34

MAGNETIC CONCEPTS: HOW ATTRACTIVE!

Subjects and Skills Science, Language Arts

Rationale Teachers often have students create webs with important vocabulary, but by using this technique students must discuss their placement of words with others and make changes, rather than simply recording the words to "get it done."

Objectives Students will (1) create a word web to connect the key concepts of magnetism.

Activity Preparation
1. Reproduce web cards on colored paper or card stock.
2. Cut the cards apart and place in separate bags or envelopes.

Activity Procedures
1. Give each group a bag of web cards.
2. Explain that this activity has many "correct answers" and what makes the group's web correct is the students' ability to defend their answers. Remind students that as long as there is a logical reason for a card's placement, it will be correct.
3. Explain the three simple rules for web cards:
   a. Students must use all of the cards (the use of the free space is optional).
   b. No more than four words may be attached to any other card—one going in, and up to three coming out. (See Figure 7.)
   c. The last, most important rule is that each member of the group must be able to explain why and how they arranged the web in that particular way.

Figure 7. Correct Web Card Placement.

4. Students should be able to defend or explain how words are linked and specifically placed. Usually by asking each of the group members about one key card, it will become obvious that the students understand their arrangement.
5. If the students cannot defend their placement of ideas, simply allow time for them to reconsider and return a few moments later.
6. Students should record their final web in their notebook.

Materials Needed (per group) Magnetism Web cards (1 set for every 2–3 students; see p. 126)

Magnetism   125

Magnetism Web Cards

Electromagnet	Free space	
North (N)	South (S)	
Magnetism	Force of attraction or repulsion between two objects	Loadstone
Greeks	Opposite poles	Temporary magnet
Force	Permanent magnets	Magnetic field
Iron	Nickel	Compass
Attract	Repel	

Lesson 35

THE STRONGMAN COMPETITION

Subjects and Skills   Science, Language Arts, Mathematics

Rationale   This activity allows students to explore a physical science concept and freely manipulate variables to solve a problem.

Objectives   Students will (1) build a working electromagnet, (2) determine the variables that control the strength of an electromagnet, and (3) combine the variables in such a way to create the strongest electromagnet possible given the supplies provided.

Activity Preparation   1. Prepare bags of materials for each group.

Activity Procedures
1. Present the problem: How can you create a magnet from a battery, a bolt, and wire?
2. Distribute the material bags to each group of students. Allow approximately 10–15 minutes for students to develop a working electromagnet.
3. Have each group share their electromagnet and discuss the similarities between the various designs. Based on these similarities, brainstorm different variables that could impact the strength of an electromagnet.
4. Each group will need to develop a data table to record their data for testing the various variables. After the data is collected, challenge each group to use their data to create the strongest electromagnet possible.
5. Each group should share their final results with the large group.
6. Discuss the post-lab questions below.

Materials Needed (per group)
Two batteries
Three bolts (with different diameters)
100 paper clips
Wire (at least 70 cm)

Post-Lab Discussion Questions
1. List the variables that have an impact on the strength of an electromagnet.
2. Which variable seemed to have the greatest impact on the strength of the electromagnet? Defend your response using data.
3. Name two common uses of electromagnets.

Lesson 36

YOU PASS!

Subjects and Skills	Science, Language Arts
Rationale	This activity allows students to investigate magnetic insulators and conductors.
Objectives	Students will (1) identify properties of magnetic insulators and conductors and (2) discover the impact of insulators and conductors on magnetic strength.

Activity Preparation

1. Cut 15 square pieces (approximately 4 cm x 4 cm) of each of the following: notebook paper, brown paper bag, foil, plastic bag, cotton cloth, and felt. Create a bag of test items with the squares, a strong magnet, and a box of paperclips.

Activity Procedures

1. Review conductors and insulators (heat or electrical). Discuss the possibility of magnetic insulators and conductors. Have students predict the properties of both magnetic insulators and conductors.
2. Introduce the activity by sharing the materials they will be testing. Have students share how they could quantify the strength of a magnetic field.
3. Distribute the material bags to groups and have them discuss and predict which will be insulators and which will be conductors. Have students develop a data table for recording these predictions, as well as their data.
4. Allow students to test each material, using just one square between the magnet and the paperclips, and record their findings. Discuss how the strength might be affected if more than one layer of material was used.
5. Students now are ready to create a new data table or add to their present one to record their ideas and predictions for this new problem.
6. Complete the data recording and discuss the post-lab questions below.

Materials Needed (per group)

Aluminum foil
Brown paper bag
Cotton cloth
Felt
Magnet
Notebook paper
Plastic bag

Post-Lab Discussion Questions

1. What properties do magnetic insulators have in common? Name two other substances you think would be magnetic insulators.
2. What properties do magnetic conductors have in common? Name two other substances you think would be magnetic conductors.
3. What did you conclude about the effect layering insulators and conductors has on the strength of a magnet?
4. When might it be important to have a magnetic insulator? Conductor?

Chapter 9

Waves, Light, and Sound

Waves, Light, and Sound Overview

This unit focuses on the study of the properties of waves, light, and sound. As with all other physical science concepts, waves, light, and sound contribute to our daily lives. Light and sound are both waves and therefore share certain properties, but they also differ in certain aspects as well. This unit provides the opportunity for students to investigate the proprieties of waves and compare and contrast two primary examples of waves: light and sound. Although students have observed water waves and light, and have heard sound, their background knowledge on the properties and behaviors of each usually is quite limited. They may or may not realize that sound can echo, but does light? Students are familiar with how water waves move, but not necessarily sound waves. This unit exposes students to both compressional (sound) waves and transverse (water) waves, which require a medium; light, which does not require a medium; and the unique qualities of each.

This unit's project asks students to use all their knowledge of waves and creating sound to design and build a musical instrument on which they can play a recognizable tune. After examining the properties of waves and how sound is created, this unit culminates with an instrument "show" and an opportunity for each student to present his or her instrument and play a song of his or her choice for his or her classmates.

Objectives for Waves, Light, and Sound

By completing the lessons in this chapter, the students will be able to:
- understand how different vibrations can create sound,
- describe the two types of waves and their properties,
- identity the properties of sound,
- build an instrument that creates sound,
- describe the nature of light and identify its properties,
- identify different light sources and how each creates light,
- describe how concave and convex mirrors reflect light,
- identify how various optic instruments use light, and
- understand the differences between color pigments and colored light.

Chapter Activities   Below is an outline of the lessons included in this chapter. Depending on the prior knowledge of your students, you can pick which activities you want to use to reinforce the concepts. I suggest that you start with the project introduction so that all of the information and concepts presented during the class will tie back into the project.

Lesson 37 is the introduction to the culminating project for this unit. It introduces the musical instrument project through the discussion of the rubric and the specific expectations of the project.

Quite simply, Lesson 38 is a demonstration of the two types of waves—*compressional* (longitudinal) and *transverse*—using a Slinky. The different parts and areas of waves will be identified and students will finish by comparing and contrasting the two types of waves. Lesson 39 is an introduction to the various properties of waves using a pan of colored water. Most students have observed a reflection of a wave, but this goes one step further by having students experience refraction and diffraction as well.

Supplies and managing equipment can be a problem in the science classroom. By setting up a rotational lab like the one in Lesson 40, students can have access to materials and equipment, but the teacher only needs one set of equipment. These rotational labs are card-based; all of the instructions can be copied onto cards and laminated for durability. These experiences are shorter and exploratory in nature.

There are many real-world examples of the Doppler Effect; most usually require large vehicles or noisy horns. Lesson 41 includes a demonstration of the Doppler Effect that is easy to conduct in a small area or classroom. Lesson 42 introduces students to the key concepts of light, optics, and color and allows students to make connections between these ideas. Students will create a concept web using movable cards. As the webs are created, students have the opportunity to discuss the concepts and their connectedness.

The rotational lab in Lesson 43 introduces and reinforces various shorter experiences using mirrors, lenses, color, and light. Students will experience the various properties of lights as well as solve some hands-on light based reflection and refraction problems. Lesson 44 is a 2-day activity centered on the students sharing their musical instruments. The first day showcases the students' instruments, while the second day has students playing recognizable tunes and sharing how their instrument produces sound.

Vocabulary for This Chapter

acoustics: the study of sound

amplitude: in a wave, the distance from the rest position of the medium to either the crest or trough

compression: in compressional waves, the dense area of the wave

compressional wave: a type of wave where matter vibrates in the same direction as the wave travels

concave: a mirror or lens in which the surface is thinner in the middle and thicker at the edges and thus curves inward

convergent: an object (mirror or lens) that brings light together

convex: a mirror or lens in which the surface is thicker in the middle and thinner at the edges and thus curves outward

crest: the highest point of a wave

diffraction: the bending of waves around a barrier

divergent: an object (mirror or lenses), which disperses or spreads out light

Doppler Effect: an increase or decrease in wave frequency; caused by motion of the source and/or motion of the observer

echo: the reflection of sound waves

lens: a piece of transparent substance having two opposite surfaces (either both curved or one curved and one plane), used in an optical device to change the convergence of light rays, as for magnification or in correcting defects of vision

medium: a material through which a wave travels

mirror: a reflecting surface, usually made of glass with a metallic or amalgam backing

optics: the study of light

pitch: the highness or lowness of a sound, determined by the frequency of the waves

prism: a transparent solid body, often having triangular bases, used for dispersing light into a spectrum or for reflecting rays of light

rarefaction: in compressional waves, the less dense area of the wave

reflection: occurs when a wave strikes an object and bounces off

refraction: the bending of waves, caused by changing their speed

rest: the position of a material when it is not in motion

shadow: the image cast when an object blocking rays of light

transverse wave: a type of wave where the medium moves at right angles to the direction the wave is traveling

trough: the lowest point of a wave

vibration: the rapid oscillation of a particle, particles, or elastic solid or surface, back and forth across a central position

wavelength: the distance from identical points on two adjacent waves

Lesson 37

YOUR OWN TUNE: THE MUSICAL INSTRUMENT PROJECT

Subjects and Skills	Science, Language Arts
Rationale	This activity encourages students to use household objects in new ways and use their creativity to create a musical instrument of their own.
Objectives	Students will (1) create a musical instrument using household objects, (2) play a recognizable tune on their instrument, and (3) explain how it creates sound.
Activity Preparation	1. Duplicate the Musical Instrument Project Rubric (p. 133) so they are ready to distribute. 2. Ready a few samples of copper pipe to demonstrate good tonal quality. It also is helpful to have a few examples of poor tonal quality—like hitting a piece of wood that is sitting on a tabletop.
Activity Procedures	1. Give each student a rubric for the Musical Instrument Project. 2. The project is worth up to 200 points, rather than the usual 100 points, although the grade can still be recorded as a percentage. Discuss each criterion with the students, providing examples and explanations for excellent, good, fair, and poor. Encourage students to give examples of each to clarify their knowledge. 3. Students are ready look for materials and brainstorm ideas for their instruments. Teachers may want to keep a junk box of recycled materials available for this project.
Materials Needed	Musical Instrument Project Rubric (p. 133)

Name: _____ Date: _____

Musical Instrument Project Rubric

Criteria	Excellent	Good	Fair	Poor
Materials Must be recycled; must not contain parts of real instruments.	30 *points* Project is homemade from recycled materials; does not contain any materials from real instruments.	25 *points* Project is homemade from mostly recycled materials; student spent less than $3 on additional materials.	15 *points* Project is homemade from mostly recycled materials; student spent more than $3 on additional materials.	0 *points* Project is store bought or contains pieces of a real instrument.
Six Notes	30 *points* Instrument can play six different notes clearly.	20 *points* Instrument can play four different notes clearly.	10 *points* Instrument can play two different notes clearly.	5 *points* Instrument can play one note clearly.
Design/Decoration	20 *points* Project is colorful, decorated, and has a theme or design unique to its creator.	15 *points* Project is colorful and decorated, but theme or design is not unique to its creator.	10 *points* Project is decorated, but is not very colorful or unique; does not have a theme or design.	5 *points* Project is minimally decorated.
Originality How many instruments were the same type (i.e., flutes, guitars, etc.)?	20 *points* Fewer than 5% of peers' instruments were similar.	15 *points* Fewer than 10% of peers' instruments were similar.	10 *points* Between 10–20% of peers' instruments were similar.	5 *points* More than 20% of peers' instruments were similar.
Recognizable Tune Points awarded based on number of notes in song.	20 *points* (Includes 5 points extra credit.) Plays a recognizable, complex song pattern, and uses six notes.	15 *points* Plays a recognizable, basic song pattern, using four to five notes.	10 *points* Plays a recognizable song pattern of three notes or less.	5 *points* Doesn't play a song, just notes.
Tonal Quality	20 *points* Instrument plays clear, smooth, musical sounds.	10 *points* Sounds are semitonal, but not musical.		5 *points* Plays basic sounds or "clunks."
Written Plans Includes materials list, measurements, drawings, and written building steps.	30 *points* Includes easy-to-read materials list, specific measurements, labeled drawings, and specific, written building steps.	20 *points* Includes materials list and specific, written building steps.	10 *points* Missing either materials list or building steps; does not include drawings or measurements.	0 *points* No plans present.
Poster Includes explanation of how instrument makes sound and how high and low pitches are created.	25 *points* Includes specific explanation of how instrument makes sound through vibration; uses words and pictures; includes how high and low pitches are created.	15 *points* Includes explanation of how instrument makes sound through vibration; does not have pictures or does not include explanation of pitches.		0 *points* Does not have poster.
Rubric	5 *points* Turned in with project.			0 *points* Rubric not returned.

Total Grade: _____
(Out of 200)

Extra Credit: You can earn one point of extra credit for each note your instrument can play beyond the required six notes.

© Prufrock Press • *Hands-On Physical Science*
This page may be photocopied or reproduced with permission for student use.

Lesson 38

WIRY WAVES

Subjects and Skills	Science
Rationale	This activity demonstrates how waves move in a visible, understandable way.
Objectives	Students will be able to (1) identify the parts of compressional and transverse waves, and (2) compare and contrast the two types of waves.
Activity Preparation	1. Ask students to brainstorm and share words related to waves. 2. Record all of the words shared so that everyone can see them. 3. Ask students to now look closely at the words and after discussing them with their group, develop categories for them. 4. Groups now can share and defend their categorizations of the words.
Activity Procedures	1. After sharing the categories of wave words, develop the idea of two distinctly different types of waves. Most students are familiar with the transverse wave. 2. Discuss the different parts of the transverse (water) wave. 3. Ask for a volunteer to help with the wave demonstration. 4. After stretching the Slinky across the room, produce a low energy transverse wave by moving the Slinky slowly up and down. 5. Have volunteers come forward to identify the crest, trough, wavelength, and amplitude of the standing wave. 6. Discuss what would change in the wave if more energy was added into its production. 7. Produce a wave with similar wavelength, but more energy (higher amplitude). Allow more volunteers to again identify the various parts, focusing on the difference in amplitude caused by energy. 8. Discuss real-world examples of transverse waves. 9. Discuss the parts of a compressional (longitudinal) wave. 10. Ask for another volunteer to demonstrate this type of wave. 11. Again, stretch the Slinky across the room. In order to create a compressional wave, pull approximately 15 coils of the Slinky together and release them. The wave becomes visible as it travels through the Slinky. 12. Have students identify the areas of compression and rarefaction. Discuss how a wavelength would be measured in this type of wave. 13. Compare this wave to a transverse wave and how the waves travel through various mediums, if mediums are needed. 14. Students are now ready to create a Venn diagram to compare and contrast compressional and transverse waves.
Materials Needed	Prepared drawings of waves Slinky

Lesson 39

WATERY WAVES ACTIVITY

Subjects and Skills	Science, Language Arts
Rationale	This activity demonstrates the properties of a wave in a simple manner.
Objectives	Students will be able to (1) create a transverse wave using water as a medium, and (2) identify examples of reflection and diffraction of waves.
Activity Preparation	1. Review transverse and longitudinal waves and their unique structures.
Activity Procedures	1. Place 2–3 drops of food coloring in each group's cookie tray. Add enough water to cover the bottom of the tray. 2. By holding the ruler perpendicular to the bottom of the pan, students should create a wave in the tray and notice how the wave moves through the tray. 3. Students should send a wave toward one of the walls of the tray and note any changes in the response of the wave. 4. Students should place the wooden blocks in the pan to create a barrier (see graphic below).

5. Students should create a wave and observe its response as it approaches and responds to the wooden blocks before drawing their observations.
6. Discuss the post-lab questions on the next page.

Materials Needed (per group)	Cookie tray (disposable aluminum trays work well and can be reused) Food coloring Ruler Water Wooden blocks

1. Considering the properties of the waves produced in this lab, were they transverse or compressional waves?

2. What did you notice about the waves as they struck the opposite side of the pan? What is this phenomenon called? When it happens to sound waves, what is it called?

3. After sending a wave into the side of the tray, what did you notice about the movement of the wave? Create a drawing to show how the wave moved.

4. Create a sketch that shows how the waves responded to the wooden blocks. What is this phenomenon called? Give at least two real-world examples of this phenomenon.

5. Tsunamis are caused when an undersea earthquake quickly moves the water, much like the way you moved your ruler in the cookie tray. Considering they can happen in the middle of the ocean, is the water in the wave that strikes the land the same water that was first moved by the earthquake's wave? Explain your reasoning.

Lesson 40

SOUND EXPLORATION ROTATIONAL LAB

Subjects and Skills	Science
Rationale	This activity allows students to have fun experiencing different ways that sound can be produced.
Objectives	Students will be able to (1) describe how sound is transmitted, and (2) identify the necessary components for sound to be produced.

Activity Preparation

1. Set up the Church Bells activity by cutting two pieces of string approximately 40 cm in length and tying a piece of string onto the bottom corners of the wire hanger.
2. Laminate the instructions for each station (or put each of the station cards into plastic sleeves to protect them).
3. Gather the materials for each of the rotational labs. Set up a station for each lab, or buckets with all of the supplies that can be taken to student desks.
4. Decide how the rotations will be handled, as free rotations or specifically ordered.

Activity Procedures

1. Have students create their own lab sheet by folding two pieces of lined paper into fours. Have them number each square 1–8. Each number represents one of the rotational labs. Students will record the information for each numbered lab in its appropriate square.
2. Before beginning their rotation, students then can set up each square of their lab paper to record their predictions (hypothesis), observations, and questions.
3. Briefly explain each station and its expectations to students. Students can make any specific notes on safety or tips for success on their lab paper for each station.

Suggestions for the Mini-Labs

After students have made their recording sheets, spending a few moments going over each station will save a lot of time once students have started their labs.

Station 1: Creating Sound: Discuss the proper way to strike the tuning forks, either using the striking mallets, palm of the hand, or rubber soles of the shoes.

Station 2: Church Bells: Demonstrate how students should wrap the string around their fingers, and remind them that the string does not go in the ears, their fingers do.

Station 3: Seeing Sounds: Mention that they will want to get close to observe this behavior.

Station 4: Can You Match It?: Usually the best tuning fork for this activity is middle C. Remind students that they are hitting a glass bottle and do not want to use too much force. They also should not blow across the bottle.

Station 6: Straw Kazoo, Part One: Remind the students to cut the straw so it has a pointed, pencil-like end. If the end is not cut properly, it is very difficult to obtain sound. Students should throw their kazoos away before moving on to their next station.

Station 7: Straw Kazoo, Part Two: Students should throw their kazoos away at this station before moving on to their next station.

Station 8: Resonance: Remind students that the tuning forks should *not* touch (this way, when the tuning fork that was not struck begins to "sing" the students know it was due to resonance).

Materials Needed (per group)	Block of wood
	Clock that ticks or small radio
	Two garbage cans for straws
	Glass bottle
	Metal spoon
	Plastic bag of water
	Two plastic cups (at least 8 ounces)
	Rubber mallets (for striking)
	Scissors
	Straws (28 larger diameter and 28 smaller diameter drinking straws)
	String
	Tuning forks (various sizes)
	Water
	Two wire coat hangers

STATION 1: CREATING SOUND

Materials: Tuning fork

Procedure:
1. Gently strike the tuning fork and observe the prongs. Record your observations.
2. Strike the prongs again. This time, place the tuning fork on your jawbone. What did you feel? Do you hear anything? What causes these sensations?
3. Draw a sound wave. Label the compression, rarefaction, and wavelength.

STATION 2: CHURCH BELLS

Materials: Wire hangers, string

Procedure:
1. Pick up the coat hanger and wrap one string around your first finger on your right hand. Wrap the other string around your first finger on your left hand.
2. Swing the hanger so it hits the edge of the desk.
3. Describe the sound that is created.
4. Now, place your fingers with the string around them in your ears, and strike the hanger on the desk. (Everyone in the group should get to try this!)
5. Describe the sound you hear now.
6. Why is this sound different?
7. How is the sound being transmitted?

STATION 3: SEEING SOUND

Materials: Plastic cup, tuning fork

Procedure:
1. Hold the open end of the plastic cup against your ear. Strike the tuning fork and very gently, touch the bottom of the cup. What do you notice? What is vibrating to create the sound?
2. Fill a plastic cup with water.
3. Predict what will happen when you place a tuning fork you have gently struck into the water.
4. Gently strike the tuning fork and touch the prongs of the tuning fork to the water. Record your observations. What causes this to happen? If you used more force, what would you expect to happen? Record your observations on your lab paper.
5. Strike the tuning fork with more force and again gently touch it to the water. Was this the expected reaction?

STATION 4: CAN YOU MATCH IT?

Materials: Tuning fork, glass bottle, metal spoon, water

Procedure:
1. Place about 1 cm of water into the bottle. Using the spoon, strike the bottle.
2. Add another centimeter of water to the bottle and strike it again. How did the pitch of the sound change?
3. Add another centimeter of water to the bottle, and strike it again. What is vibrating to create this sound?
4. Strike the tuning fork at your station. How would you need to change the water level in your bottle to try and match the frequency of the tuning fork?
5. Adjust the water level to try and match the frequency. What height of water seemed to match the frequency the best? Is this what you predicted? Explain.

STATION 5: DOES IT MATTER?

Materials: Block of wood, plastic bag filled with water, clock that ticks or small radio

Procedure:
1. Make a prediction about the clarity of sound as it travels through air, water, and wood. Which will allow the clearest sound? Why do you think so?
2. Hold the block of wood up to your ear. Place the clock against the wooden block. How easy was it to hear through the wood? Was this what you expected? Explain.
3. Next hold the plastic bag of water up to your ear. Again, place the clock against the bag. Compared to the wooden block, was it easier or more difficult to hear?
4. Make a drawing of the molecules in solids, liquids, and gases. How does this drawing explain how sound travels differently through the different states?

STATION 6: STRAW KAZOO: PART ONE

Materials: Scissors, soft drink straws (large diameter), ruler, garbage can for straws

Procedure:
1. Flatten the end of a straw by chewing on the end.
2. Cut the end of the straw so it has a pointed end like a pencil.

3. Record the length of your straw. Blow forcefully on the cut end of the straw to create a sound.
4. The wavelength of the sound you produced was the twice the straw length. Record the wavelength.
5. Starting at the uncut end of the straw, snip off 2 cm of straw. Trying blowing into the straw again.
6. How did the pitch change as you snipped off pieces of the straw?
7. Throw away your kazoo.

STATION 7: STRAW KAZOO: PART TWO

Materials: Scissors, ruler, straws (smaller diameter), garbage can for straws

Procedure:
1. Be sure you have completed Straw Kazoo Part 1 first!
2. Think about what your other straw looked like. Compare this straw to the other one. How is this straw like the other?
3. If you created a kazoo from this straw, how do you think the sound will be different from the sound produced by the straw in Part 1? Explain.
4. Create another kazoo from this size straw that is the same length as the straw in Part 1.
5. Again, snip off the ends of the straw to hear its effect on pitch.
6. How does this kazoo differ from the other kazoo?
7. Throw away your kazoo.

STATION 8: RESONANCE

Materials: Two tuning forks with the same frequency

Procedure:
1. Strike one tuning fork. Bring it close to the second tuning fork (but do not let them touch).
2. Listen to the second tuning fork (bring it close to your ear).
3. Record your observations.
4. This is an example of resonance. Explain why this happens.

Lesson 41

TIME FLIES DEMONSTRATION

Subjects and Skills	Science
Rationale	This activity demonstrates phenomena that students can encounter daily.
Objectives	Students will (1) identify the Doppler Effect, (2) explain why it takes place, and (3) provide examples of this effect in their everyday experiences.

Activity Preparation

1. Prepare the Doppler Effect apparatus by securely tying the string to the handle on the alarm clock.
2. Locate two video clip examples of the Doppler Effect (one for a slow-moving object like a train, the other for a fast-moving object like a racecar). There are many short clips available on the Internet.

Activity Procedures

1. Begin by sharing the Doppler Effect video clip with the students. Ask them to explain what they are hearing. For example (if the video is of a train), did the train change its horn as it went by the observer? Would it make a difference where the observer stood? What if they were riding on the train? (There is no change because you are traveling with the sound wave.) How would they express the change? Create interest and questions in this pitch change and how it is created.
2. The train's pitch change is, of course, an example of the Doppler Effect, which easily can be demonstrated using an alarm clock on a string. Sound the alarm and allowing about one meter of string, swing the alarm clock in a circle above your head. (Make sure you have enough room and the string is secure.)
3. Listen to the pitch of the alarm clock. Describe what is heard. How is this similar to the sound heard in the video clip? What is causing the pitch change? Where is the pitch higher? Lower? Does this pitch change match that of the video clip?
4. Review wavelength and its effect on pitch; if the students experienced the straw kazoo rotational labs, this can be discussed by relating the length of the straw to the pitch created in the kazoo lab. Using the kazoo example, explain that as the wavelength got shorter, the pitch got higher. Therefore, as the pitch of the alarm clock changes to higher, the wavelengths are getting shorter. As the pitch is lower, the wavelengths are longer. Knowing this, what could be causing the shorter wavelengths in the clock example? The video clip example? (The clock is moving towards us, so the sound waves are compressed, as it moves away, the waves are spread out, with a longer wavelength, so it has a lower pitch.)

5. Compare the alarm clock to the video clip. What is causing the higher pitch in the video clip? The lower pitch?

6. Discuss changing one variable in the swinging clock: the speed of the circling. Students should predict how this would impact the pitches heard, as well as any change in the Doppler Effect. Students should defend their predictions during the discussion.

7. Conduct the demonstration again, swinging it faster to confirm the predictions of the students. How does this relate to real-world situations?

8. Show a video clip with a faster moving object. Although the effect is still obvious, how has it changed? What is causing the change?

9. Students now can draw examples of the Doppler Effect showing the waves and pitch changes, such as those in Figure 8.

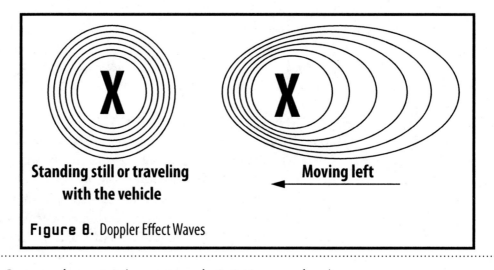

Standing still or traveling with the vehicle

Moving left

Figure 8. Doppler Effect Waves

Materials Needed   Strong nylon string (approximately 2–2 ½ meters long)
Video clips of the Doppler Effect
Wind up alarm clock with a handle on the top

Lesson 42

LIGHT AND COLOR CONNECTIONS

Subjects and Skills	Science, Language Arts
Rationale	This activity will allow students make connections between the key concepts of light, optics, and color.
Objectives	Students will be able to (1) create a web of key words associated with light, color, and optics, and (2) defend the placement of each concept.
Activity Preparation	1. Reproduce web cards on colored paper or cardstock. 2. Cut the cards apart and place in separate bags or envelopes.
Activity Procedures	1. Give each group a set of web cards. 2. Explain that what makes the webs correct is the students' ability to defend their answers. Remind students that as long as there is a logical reason for the card's placement, it will be correct. See the guidelines for web cards in Lesson 34 (p. 125). 3. Once the students have placed the cards, they should be able defend or explain how words and concepts are linked and specifically placed. If the students cannot defend their placement of ideas, simply allow time for them to reconsider. 4. Once the webs have been confirmed and defended, students can record their final web in their notebook.
Materials Needed (per group)	Web cards (1 set for every 2–3 students; p. 146)

Light Web Cards

Concave	Convex	Free space
Convergent	Divergent	Disperses or spreads out
Brings together	Lens	Secondary (orange, purple, green)
Transverse wave	Shadow	Primary (red, blue, yellow)
Mirror	Optics	Primary (magenta, yellow, cyan)
Light	Color	Refraction
Prism	Reflection	Diffraction

Lesson 43

LIGHT AND COLOR ROTATIONAL LAB

Subjects and Skills	Science, Language Arts, Mathematics
Rationale	This activity allows students to experience different properties of light and color and explain observations by applying their knowledge of light and color.
Objectives	Students will be able to (1) compare and contrast the structure of convex and concave mirrors, (2) explain how light waves respond to each, (3) identify how light and colors combine to create different colors, and (4) identify how optical instruments work.

Activity Preparation

1. Gather the materials for each of the rotational labs. Set up a station for each lab, or buckets with all the supplies that can be taken to student desks.
2. Set up the Sources of Light station by creating two sets of sorting cards by duplicating the cards onto cardstock and cutting them apart.
3. Set up the Seeing Around Corners station by creating the laser puzzle box in an empty shoebox as shown in Figure 9.
4. Set up the Combining Color station by attaching one theater gel on the end of each flashlight using a rubber band.

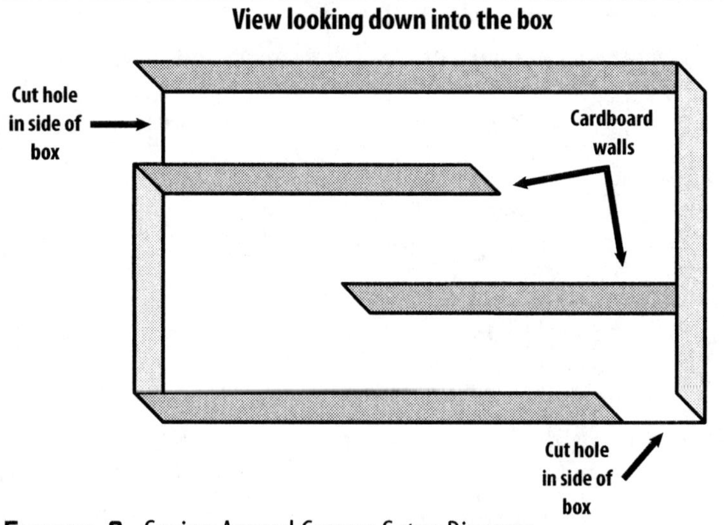

Figure 9. Seeing Around Corners Setup Diagram

Activity Procedures

1. Have students create their own lab sheet by folding two pieces of lined paper into fours. Have them number each square 1–7 to represent one of the rotational labs. Students will record their predictions, observations, and questions for each numbered lab in its appropriate square.

2. Briefly explain each station and its expectations to students. Students can make any specific notes on safety on their lab paper for each station.

Suggestions for the Light Mini-Labs

After students have made their lab sheets, spending a few moments going over each station will save a lot of time once students have started their labs.

Station 3: Make Your Own Kaleidoscope: Demonstrate how the sample microscope slides were taped together. This is the one step that often confuses students.

Station 5: Seeing Around Corners: Care should be taken with the laser pointer, as well as the mirrors. Laser pointers, although seemingly harmless, produce a form of concentrated light. Student should avoid looking directly into the light or shining the light into another student's eye. Mirrors can break if dropped; if a mirror is dropped and broken, the teacher should sweep up the broken glass.

Station 6: Perplexing Pigments: Although tempera paint is usually washable, students will want to avoid getting it on their clothing.

Materials Needed (for 7 groups)

Black electrical tape
Cardboard or stiff paper
Clay
Colored pieces for kaleidoscope (beads, sequins, etc.)
Colored theater light gels (red, cyan, magenta; you can usually obtain these from your school's drama group or local high schools)
One clear film canister per student (can be obtained at film processing locations)
One dark film canister per student
Three flashlights
Laser pointer
Microscope slides (three per student)
Five to six small mirrors (no smaller than 3" x 5")
Paper clips
Penny
Plastic cup that is not clear (at least 8 ounces)
Plastic wrap
Pointillism picture example
Silver spoon (large and shiny)
Shoebox with lid
Styrofoam cup (at least 8 ounces)
Tape
Toothpicks
Wax paper
White paper

STATION 1: FIND THE FISH

Materials: Penny, cup of water, plastic cup (that is not clear)

Procedure:
1. Place the penny in the bottom of the cup against the side.
2. Keeping your eye on the penny, lower your head until you can just see it over the rim of the cup.
3. Without moving your head, add water to the cup.
4. Record your observations.

Questions:
1. Explain what property of light is taking place in this station.
2. It takes a skilled fisherman to be able to spear a fish underwater. Using your observations from this station, explain why this task is difficult.

STATION 2: THE GREAT SPOON

Materials: Large shiny silver spoon

Procedure:
1. The large spoon at this station easily can be used as a concave and convex mirror.
2. Make a drawing of the spoon and label the concave and convex sides.
3. Examine your reflection created on both sides of the spoon. Record your observations.
4. Move the spoon closer and further away. Does the image change?

Questions:
1. Does the distance from the spoon make a difference in the image? Explain.
2. Some mirrors are convergent, while others are divergent. Explain what both of these words mean, and which side of the spoon represents each.

STATION 3: MAKE YOUR OWN KALEIDOSCOPE

Materials: Two film canisters, one clear, one dark; three microscope slides; black electrical tape; colored pieces (beads, sequins, etc.); paper clip; plastic wrap

Procedure:
1. Lay the microscope slides side-by-side with the long sides almost touching.
2. Carefully place pieces of black electrical tape on the slides to hold them together.
3. Then completely cover the top side of the slides with the tape.
4. Using the slides, fold the two ends together to make a triangle tube.
5. Place another piece of black electrical tape on the edges to hold the tube in its shape.
6. Using the end of the paper clip carefully poke a hole in the end of the dark film canister.
7. Carefully slide the triangle tube into the dark canister.
8. Cover the open end of the dark film canister with plastic wrap. Tape down the plastic wrap.
9. Place a few colored items into the clear film canister.
10. Slide the clear film canister over the end of the dark film canister.
11. Tape the two canisters together.

Questions:
1. What property of light does this station demonstrate?
2. Why did you need to use black electrical tape? Would other colored tape have worked? Explain.

STATION 4: SOURCES OF LIGHT

Materials: Sources of Light Sorting Cards

Procedure:
1. The items listed on the sorting cards represent various ways that light can be produced.
2. Keep in mind that sources of light can be categorized as either natural or artificial. Discuss how each item on the sorting cards produces light.
3. Make a chart of the natural and artificial sources.
4. Defend the categorization of each item.

Questions:
1. Record your chart and defenses.
2. List two other ways that light is produced.

STATION 5: SEEING AROUND CORNERS

Materials: Seeing Around Corners puzzle box with lid, laser pointer, mirrors, clay

Procedure:
1. In the past, mirrors have been used to "move" light into areas that are dark. Your challenge for this station is create a pathway so light can travel into one hole in the box, and come out the other.
2. You are welcome to use as many of the mirrors as needed. They can be supported using clay.
3. When you feel you have a successful set up, close the shoebox, and using the laser, test your box.
4. Make adjustments as needed until you can successfully move light through the box.

Questions:
1. Make a drawing that shows your final set-up, including walls and mirror placement.
2. What variables had to be considered in order to be successful?
3. The ancient Egyptians used a similar technique in the tunnels of their pyramids while they were being constructed. Using scientific vocabulary, explain how this allowed them to light their tunnels very deep into the pyramid.

STATION 6: PERPLEXING PIGMENTS

Materials: Toothpicks; wax paper; tempera paints: red, blue, and yellow; white paper; pointillism picture

Procedure:
1. Examine the picture provided. This is an example of an artistic technique known as pointillism. Record your observations, including how you think these types of pictures are created.
2. You have been provided with the three primary pigment colors. It is your challenge to create a group picture in the style of pointillism.
3. Your picture should have areas of primary and secondary color; however, you should not mix any colors to obtain the secondary colors. The layering of primary colors can create secondary colors. Your eyes will combine the two colors to create the secondary colors.
4. Discuss what your group would like to paint and sketch the outline of your painting.
5. Place a small amount of each color on your waxed paper. Using the toothpicks, and small points of paint, create your painting.
6. Leave your painting in a safe place to dry.

Questions:
1. What are the three secondary colors? Explain what combinations of primary colors create each.
2. What was most challenging about creating the secondary colors?

Materials: 3 flashlights with colored gels, large Styrofoam cup

Procedure:
1. The three flashlights are covered with gels. These three colors are the three primary colors of light.
2. You will be testing the different combination of the primary colors of light. Create a data table that can be used to record all of the different combinations of the three colors (including all three colors together).
3. Test the various combinations of light by shining the flashlights into the Styrofoam cup. Record the colors that are created in each situation.

Questions:
1. How are the primary colors of light different from primary pigment colors? Using your knowledge of reflected light, explain why this may be so.
2. Gels are commonly used in theater lighting. In order to create all the colors of the rainbow, what would be the fewest number of lights a theater would need to purchase? Explain your answer and how to use the different gels to create all of the rainbow colors.

Sources of Light Sorting Cards

Lightbulb	Campfire	Fireworks
Sum	Forest fire	Candle
Flashlight	Propane or gas flame	Glow in the dark stickers
Stars	Headlights on a car	Glow in the dark tube bracelet or necklace
Firefly	Television screen	Fluorescent bulb
Laser		

Lesson 44

SHOW US YOUR MUSICAL INSTRUMENT

Subjects and Skills	Science, Oral Presentation Skills, Language Arts
Rationale	This activity allows students to provide positive feedback for their peers and showcase their projects.
Objectives	Students will (1) critique classmates' musical instruments on three different criteria, (2) provide positive feedback about other instruments, and (3) demonstrate the different notes their instrument can produce by playing a recognizable tune.
Activity Preparation	1. Optional: Send home invitations for the parents to attend the show.
Activity Procedures	1. Day 1 of the activity is the musical instrument show. Begin this day by assigning a number to each student to record on his or her feedback sheet.
	2. Distribute the Musical Instrument Evaluation Sheet (pp. 155–156). This paper, along with the student's written plans, will stay beside the instruments as the students rotate from desk to desk, recording their comments.
	3. Before beginning the rotations, discuss each of the three criteria students will be evaluating: creativity of design, originality of design, and the ease of understanding the written plans. Students will be rating instruments on a scale of 1–10. A perfect score is a 10, while a 1 would be used for someone who did not at all meet the requirements of the project.
	4. The last column is available for specific and positive feedback for the instrument. It is expected that each student will make a positive comment for each project.
	5. Have each student rate his or her own instruments on the first line of the evaluation sheet.
	6. The second day of the activity involves the students' performances. As students get ready to play their instrument, they should come to the performance area. Once there, they will briefly share how they made their instrument, then play their tune. Ask the class to identify the tune that was played.
	7. The presenter should then share his or her poster describing how his or her instrument creates sound.
	8. Once all of the instruments have been played, students can begin working on the questions on the second page of the evaluation sheet.
Materials Needed	Musical Instrument Evaluation Sheet (pp. 155–156)

Name: _____ Date: _____

Musical Instrument Evaluation Sheet

Your Number	Creativity of Design (1–10)	Originality of Instrument (1–10)	Easy to Follow Plans (1–10)	Comments

Name: _____ Date: _____

Musical Instrument Evaluation

Answer each question in paragraph form.

Did you enjoy this project? Explain why you enjoyed it or not.

What was most challenging about this project? Why?

If you could do your project over again what would you do differently? Why?

Chapter 10

Nuclear Energy

Nuclear Energy Overview

This unit focuses on a town hall meeting debate. The small town of Ketchikan has received a proposal from a nuclear power company that would like to build a power plant to supply the majority of power for the town and at least half the state. Should the company be allowed to build the plant? What should be considered before making a decision? After providing information on nuclear fission, fusion, and half-lives, this unit concludes in the town debate and the final decision. Unlike the majority of the physical science concepts, most students do not come into the classroom knowing a lot about nuclear energy, its production, benefits, or drawbacks. If students do have prior knowledge quite often it is a sensationalized perspective, focusing only on the negative side of this energy source. This unit helps students fill the gaps in their knowledge, as well as focuses on a more balanced informational approach to the issue.

Objectives for Nuclear Energy

By completing the activities in this chapter, the students will be able to:
- understand how nuclear energy is produced,
- describe the fission and fusion process,
- identify the benefits and drawbacks of nuclear energy and nuclear power plants, and
- explain the process of radioactive half-life decay.

Chapter Activities

Below is an outline of the lessons included in this chapter. Depending on the prior knowledge of your students, you can pick which activities you want to use to reinforce the concepts. I suggest that you start with the project introduction so that all of the information and concepts presented during the class will tie back into the project.

Lesson 45 is an introduction to the project for this unit. This unit's project has students taking on individual personas in order to actively participate in a town hall debate. Students will be introduced to the expectations of the project and the standards for the town hall debate.

In Lesson 46 students become well-informed citizens as they research nuclear power. 3 Facts and a Fib is known to be a popular party game; it also can liven up a classroom as students challenge each other in Lesson 47 to find the fib in the four statements about nuclear fission and fusion. Lesson 48 is a simulated half-life lab experience. It walks the students through the steps of radioactive decay as particles change from parent products to daughter products.

The long awaited debate takes place in Lesson 49. Students arrive in persona ready to question the aspects of nuclear power and state their opinions regarding the placement of a nuclear power plant. Will the townspeople decide to allow the company to build the power plant?

Vocabulary for This Chapter

alpha particle: a particle of nuclear radiation emitted from a decaying atomic nucleus; has a charge of 2+, an atomic mass of 4, and is the largest, slowest, and least penetrating form of radiation

beta particle: a negatively charged electron or positively charged positron emitted from a decaying atomic nucleus; beta particles are faster moving and more penetrating than alpha particles

daughter product: the product created in a nuclear reaction

fission: a nuclear reaction in which a nucleus of an atom is split, releasing energy

fusion: a nuclear reaction in which nuclei combine to form a more massive nuclei, releasing energy

gamma rays: high frequency electromagnetic waves that travel at the speed of light, have no mass, or charge, and are the most penetrating form of radiation

half-life: the amount of time required for one-half of the nuclides in a sample of radioactive isotope to decay

nuclear decay: the process in which an unstable atomic nucleus loses energy by emitting radiation in the form of particle or electromagnetic waves

radioactive substance: an unstable substance whose nucleus breaks down and gives off particles, radiation, and energy

Lesson 45

THE GREAT DEBATE

Subjects and Skills	Science, Language Arts
Rationale	This activity builds excitement for the town hall debate in which students have the opportunity to take on other personas and evaluate a controversial topic.
Objectives	Students will be able to (1) describe the purpose of the town debate and (2) express characteristics of their persona for the debate.
Activity Preparation	1. Prepare the personality cards. Although most cards can be either male or female, there are a few that are gender specific and designated as such in the title.
Activity Procedures	1. Give each student a copy of the Town Hall Debate Project Rubric (pp. 160–161). The project is worth up to 150 points, rather than the usual 100 points, although the grade still can be recorded as a percentage. Discuss each criterion with the students, especially reinforcing that students must conduct the interviews themselves (no filling out of surveys) and that the essay must be persuasive, not informative.
	2. Walk around the room asking students to pick their persona card.
	3. Students now are prepared to begin investigating their persona, as well as the aspects of nuclear power as they progress through the unit.
Materials Needed	Town Hall Debate Project Rubric (pp. 160–161) Persona cards (pp. 162–163)

Town Hall Debate Project Rubric

Criteria	Excellent	Good	Fair	Poor
Research Shows depth of research on nuclear energy, including how it is produced, its benefits and drawbacks; research is nonjudgmental, nonbiased, and factual; includes bibliography.	*20 points* Research explains how nuclear energy is produced, its benefits and drawbacks; research is nonjudgmental, nonbiased, and factual; includes accurate bibliography.	*15 points* Research explains how nuclear energy is produced, its benefits and drawbacks; few facts are judgmental in nature; includes accurate bibliography.	*12 points* Research does not explain how nuclear energy is produced or is missing its benefits and drawbacks; several facts are judgmental; bibliography is inaccurate, but present.	*0 points* Missing important facts or all research is completely judgmental in nature, or missing bibliography.
Interview Questions Seven questions that gather perceptions and knowledge about nuclear power.	*10 points* Chooses seven good questions, appropriate to gather perceptions and knowledge about nuclear power.	*8 points* Has five to six good questions, or seven that are not as focused on obtaining pertinent information.	*6 points* Has less than five questions.	*0 points* No interview questions present.
Interview Summaries Three summaries, one for each interview, that provide key points of interviews.	*30 points* Three summaries that provide key points from each interviewee.	*15 points* Three summaries that miss a few key points or two good summaries.	*12 points* One good summary or two to three summaries missing most key points.	*0 points* No interview summaries present.
Position Essay Content Includes information from research and interviews to support position on nuclear power.	*10 points* Includes appropriate information from multiple research and interview sources to support position.	*8 points* Includes appropriate information from two research and interview sources to support position.	*6 points* Includes appropriate information from one source to support position.	*0 points* Support is not given for student's position.
Essay Correctness	*10 points* Information presented on nuclear power is correct.	*8 points* Information presented on nuclear power is correct, with one minor error.		*0 points* Information presented has multiple errors.

Name: _____ Date: _____

Criteria	Excellent	Good	Fair	Poor
Essay Persuasiveness Persuasive, focuses on debate position; information is factual and supportive; addresses nonsupportive arguments.	10 *points* Strong persuasive point made; at least four documented, factual reasons for position; nonsupportive points are discussed and refuted.	8 *points* Persuasive point made; three documented, factual reasons provided; nonsupportive points are not discussed and refuted.	6 *points* Weak persuasive point made; two or fewer documented, factual reasons provided; nonsupportive points are discussed and refuted.	0 *points* Essay is not persuasive or no supporting points for position given.
Essay Voice	10 *points* Written in voice of debate persona without stating persona directly; areas of support or concern are clear and relate to persona.	8 *points* Essay reflects persona to some degree, but lacks true voice in its persuasiveness.		0 *points* No voice in the essay; written from student's point of view.
Debate Content	20 *points* Content shared is correct.	15 *points* Content shared had one error, but it did not affect impact.		0 *points* Blatant inaccuracies in content shared.
Debate Participation Participated in debate; asked or answered questions; made educated statements.	20 *points* Sought opportunities to speak; asked or answered questions; made educated statements.	15 *points* Participated in debate as necessary; asked or answered questions; made educated statements.	12 *points* Participated in debate; asked or answered questions; seemed confused at times by content.	0 *points* Did not participate.
Debate Personality Persona was shown by questions asked, content shared, and personality/clothing incorporated.	10 *points* Persona was obvious and supported by questions asked, content shared, and personality/clothing incorporated.	8 *points* Persona was somewhat obvious; questions related to persona.	6 *points* Persona was slightly obvious by the questions asked.	0 *points* Persona was not clear.

Total Grade: _____
(Out of 150)

Town Hall Persona Cards

Female Citizen

Wife of farmer's son; currently living with farmer; husband is unemployed.
Age: 38, married, no children

Male Citizen

Child of a farmer; he and his wife are currently living with parents because he is unemployed.
Age: 42, married, no children

Female Citizen

Farmer's wife, currently living with her parents.
Age: 38, widowed, 2 children

Citizen

Currently travels from home to home of relatives in town.
Age: 34, no children, single

Female Citizen

Farmer's wife; has sold farm recently and now lives in town to be close to family.
Age: 74, married, 14 grandchildren

Male Citizen

Farmer; has sold farm recently and now lives in town to be close to family.
Age: 74, married, 14 grandchildren

Citizen

Farmer, running farm alone; very unsuccessful; is about to lose the farm.
Age: 41, not married, no children

Citizen

Farmer; has lived on farm since childhood; farm is 5 km from the proposed nuclear site.
Age: 36, married, 5 children

Citizen

Lives in town, parents are teachers; has a boyfriend/girlfriend.
Age: 16, not married, no children

Citizen

Child of a farmer; goes to school in town; has two older brothers and two younger brothers; loves to ride horses.
Age: 14

Citizen

Mayor; all children have grown and moved away, lives in town, is up for reelection.
Age: 58, married, 3 children

Citizen

Elementary science teacher; loves the job.
Age: 24, not married, no children

Citizen

Doctor; lives in town, has been the town doctor since graduating from medical school.
Age: 43, not married, no children

Citizen

Storeowner; has lived in town for 3 years; owns a very successful pharmacy.
Age: 32, not married, no children

Citizen

Farmer; married, has owned farm for 30 years; farm is 3 km from proposed nuclear site.
Age: 54, married, no children

Citizen

Store worker; is very unhappy with job in the pharmacy; does not feel pay is good enough.
Age: 26, not married, no children

Citizen

High school science teacher; has worked at school for 32 years.
Age: 54, not married, no children

Citizen

One of farmer's 14 grandchildren; would like a car for 16th birthday, but family cannot afford to buy one.
Age: 15

Plant Personnel

Architect; 15 years of experience; will live 350 km away from plant.
Age: 35, married, two children

Plant Personnel

Mechanical engineer; 10 years of experience; will live 200 km away from plant.
Age: 41, not married, no children

Plant Personnel

Architect's assistant; 1 year of experience; will live 100 km away from plant.
Age: 25, not married, no children

Plant Personnel

Assistant foreman of power plant; 4 years of experience; will live in town.
Age: 29, married, one child

Plant Personnel

Public relations director; 20 years of experience; will live in town.
Age: 52, married, three children

Plant Personnel

Spokesman for plant personnel; 8 years of experience; will live 200 km away from plant.
Age: 35, married, two children

Plant Personnel

Foreman of power plant; 20 years of experience; will live in town.
Age: 45, married, four children

Plant Personnel

Mechanical engineer; 5 years of experience; will live 200 km away from plant.
Age: 32, married, no children

Plant Personnel

Public relations assistant director; 5 years of experience; will live 300 km from town.
Age: 30, married, no children

Plant Personnel

Mechanical engineer; 5 years of experience; will live in town.
Age: 45, married, five children

Lesson 46

Subjects and Skills Science, Language Arts, Research Skills

Rationale This activity helps students become better informed for their position in the town hall debate.

Objectives Students will be able to describe (1) the processes of fission and fusion, (2) the benefits of fission and fusion, and (3) the drawbacks of using fission and fusion.

Activity Preparation

1. Make arrangements for access to computers, usually for 1–2 days at the beginning of the unit. If computer or Internet access is not available, resources can be located online, printed, and brought into the classroom.
2. Gather examples of effective printed interviews (that include questions and responses) from magazines or various Web sites.

Activity Procedures

1. In order to prepare for the town hall debate, students will need to become more knowledgeable in how nuclear power is created, along with its benefits and drawbacks. Ask students to step into the shoes of their assigned persona for a moment. For the debate, students will need to know about fission; however, if you are conducting Lesson 47, they also will need to know about fusion.
2. Ask students what questions they would need to know in order to be better-informed participants in the town hall debate. The citizens may focus on the benefits and drawbacks, while the plant personnel may need to know how the plant produces power.
3. Record the questions as students share them. Some questions will have factual answers, while others may be answered by perceptions or opinions.
4. Once students have shared all of their questions, have them work with a partner to briefly discuss what methods might be best for obtaining the different answers. Have various pairs share their ideas.
5. After discussing the options, students should now be able to prioritize and narrow the questions down to the 10 questions that will provide the best information.
6. Students then can separate the 10 questions based on the method they will use to obtain the information. The more information the students have, the better prepared they will be for the town hall debate.
7. At this time, students are ready to begin designing their interview questions. Some of the 10 important questions are usually based on opinion. Students' interview questions can be both factual and opinionated in nature. (Of course,

they may need to be reminded that some people may not know how a nuclear plant works, so that question may be better for the research list.) Once students embrace the idea of interviewing people, they often begin to look for experts in the field, who can provide wonderful insight into their persona.

8. For students who do not have experience using interviews to obtain information, students can work in pairs looking over the interview examples, then process which examples seemed to be effective in obtaining information. Discuss with these students how questions should be structured in an open-ended way.

9. Before leaving the class, students should have two lists of questions: those that will be researched the following day, and those that will be asked of others through interviews. The interview questions should not simply be surveys in which the responder records his or her answers on the paper. Instead, students should ask the questions and record the responses provided.

10. The research, interview questions, and answers provided make up a significant part of the project rubric.

11. Note: The plant personnel will need some time during the research phase in order to plan their presentation, including who will make the drawings, who will speak on each aspect, and so on.

....

Materials Needed   Sample interviews
(per group)   Internet access or printed resources

Lesson 47

Subjects and Skills	Science, Language Arts
Rationale	This activity helps students use their knowledge of fission and fusion in a non-traditional way and become better informed for their position in the town hall debate.
Objectives	Students will be able to describe (1) the process of fission and fusion, (2) the benefits of each, and (3) the drawbacks of each.
Activity Preparation	1. Students should have conducted their research and interviews on the nuclear energy options: fission and fusion.
Activity Procedures	1. Students need to work with a partner for this activity.

Activity Procedures (continued)

2. Allow approximately 10 minutes for both partners to share and discuss their research and interview results. They should focus on any contradictory information or surprising responses.
3. Using this information, each pair will choose a total of six facts and two fibs from their research (focusing on how energy is produced in fission and fusion, as well as the benefits and drawbacks of using each). The goal is to try and make the fibs sound realistic, so that their classmates will find the riddle difficult.
4. Once they have chosen their facts and fibs, students can create two different riddles, each with three facts and one fib.
5. Each group will take turns standing and sharing one of their riddles. The statements can be read numbered 1–4, so the audience can place their "fib" vote using their hands. If there is descent about which statement is the fib, have various audience members support their votes using facts from their research. It is completely possible there is more than one fib based on the exact wording that was used in the statement. Be prepared for lots of discussion, as students really enjoy this activity.

Lesson 48

Subjects and Skills	Science, Language Arts, Mathematics
Rationale	This activity allows students to simulate the process of radioactive half-lives.
Objectives	Students will be able to (1) identify radioactive parent and daughter products and (2) calculate half-lives of various radioactive substances.
Activity Preparation	1. Gather materials for each group.
Activity Procedures	1. Introduce or review the presence of radioactive elements and their unstable nature. Although students often understand that these elements release radiation and can be dangerous, they do not always understand radioactive decay is a change at the atomic level, so this will need to be discussed based on the intended depth of the lesson (particle decays, nuclear reaction formulas, etc.).
	2. In this lab, students will be simulating the life and death of a clam and how Carbon-14 can be used to date it.
	3. Students need to count their materials, making sure they are starting with 100 pennies. The heads side will represent an atom of the radioactive isotope Carbon-14, and the tails side will represent an atom of its daughter product, Carbon-12.
	4. Carbon is a building block of all living things, and all living things have some Carbon-14 mixed with the Carbon-12 within them. For this situation, our clam has 100 atoms of Carbon-14 in it. Students will need to set up their "clam" in the shoebox by placing all 100 pennies heads side up in the bottom of the box, then replacing the lid.
	5. The clam eventually grows old and dies on the bottom of the sea floor. Time passes, 5,730 years to be exact. (The half-life of carbon is 5,730 years. Each time the students shake the box, it represents another 5,730 years of passed time.) As time has passed, some of the Carbon-14 has begun to decay. To simulate time passing, students will need to give one strong shake (up and down) of the box.
	6. Upon opening the box, some of the Carbon-14 atoms have changed to its daughter product Carbon-12—designated by the tails side of the penny showing. Students need to count and remove the changed pennies and replace them with paperclips. These paperclips represent the daughter product that was created. (Therefore, the students see that no matter disappeared, it simply changed forms.)

7. Students should note the amount of time that has passed, the amount of daughter product created, and the amount of remaining radioactive isotope.

8. Students should continue their shaking their box and recording half-lives, each time counting and removing the newly created atoms, and completing their data tables until all atoms have been changed to the daughter product.

9. Students should now be ready to create a graph of their data and answer the post-lab questions on the lab sheet.

Materials Needed
(per group)

100 paper clips
100 pennies
Shoebox
It's a Girl! We Have a Daughter! Lab (pp. 169–171)

It's a Girl! We Have a Daughter! Lab

SITUATION

Carbon is a building block of all living things, and all living things have both the radio-active isotope Carbon-14 and the stable Carbon-12 within them. For our lab today, we will be looking at the life and death of a simulated prehistoric clam. Many years ago, a happy clam was living its life on the prehistoric ocean floor. Sadly, it died. This lab begins just a few moments before its death.

PROCEDURE

1. In this simulation, the shoebox represents your clam, and the pennies represent carbon atoms. A penny with its head showing represents a radioactive Carbon-14 atom, while the tails side of a penny represents the stable Carbon-12 atom.
2. To create our living "clam," place 100 pennies heads side up in the bottom of the shoebox. This represents the 100 Carbon-14 atoms that the clam has in it while it happily wanders the ocean floor. Place the lid back on your box.
3. When the clam dies, Carbon-14 begins its decay process. As time passes, more and more Carbon-14 atoms will decay into the daughter product: Carbon-12. We can simulate time passing with one strong shake up and down of our "clam." This shake represents 5,730 years of time passing.
4. Open your clam and examine the contents. Some of the Carbon-14 atoms have changed to their daughter product Carbon-12 (designated by the tails side of the penny showing).
5. Remove the tails-side-up pennies from the clam. Count the changed pennies and record the number in your data table.
6. To make it easier to identify the stable Carbon-12 atoms in future shakes, we will be using paperclips to represent Carbon-12. Therefore, replace each penny you removed with a paperclip.
7. Another 5,730 years passes with another strong shake of the clam. Repeat your process of removing the Carbon-12 daughter atoms, counting them and recording their numbers in the data table. Remember to replace them with paperclips!
8. Repeat this process until there are no longer any radioactive Carbon-14 atoms left in the clam.
9. Create a graph that shows the relationship between the number of decayed atoms and the number of trials or shakes of the clam.

Name: _____ Date: _____

Number of Shakes	Total Number of Years Passed (5,730 years/ shake)	Carbon-14 Atoms Present	Carbon-12 Atoms Present	Percentage of Carbon-14 Present	Percentage of Carbon-12 Present	Ratio of Parent to Daughter Product
0	5,730 years	100	0	100%	0%	1:0
1						
2						
3						
4						
5						
6						
7						
8						
9						
10						

Name: _____ Date: _____

1. Carbon has a half-life of 5,730 years. Based on your data, why is half-life an appropriate word to describe the results your observed?

_____

_____

_____

_____

2. Using scientific laws, explain why it was important to replace the Carbon-12 tails pennies with paperclips, rather than just removing them.

_____

_____

_____

_____

3. Once-living organisms can be "dated" using radioactive dating. This is done by comparing the percentage of daughter product in an organism to the amount of parent product in the same organism. Use your data to date how old a clam would be if it has ¼ Carbon-14 and ¾ Carbon-12 in its shell. Explain how you calculated this information.

_____

_____

_____

_____

4. Carbon-14 dating has a limit of approximately 60,000 years. Explain why it would not be effective for dating organisms that are more than 60,000 years old.

_____

_____

_____

_____

Lesson 49

THE GREAT DEBATE

Subjects and Skills	Science, Language Arts, Oral Presentation Skills
Rationale	This activity allows students to experience nuclear power in a real-world situation.
Objectives	Students will be able to (1) examine the issue of nuclear power from different viewpoints and (2) make an educated decision about its use.

Activity Preparation

1. Remind students the day before the debate that they should not only come to class ready to participate, but enter the room in persona.
2. Discuss the expectations for behavior the following day. Students sometimes get into their persona so much that they forget that they are in a classroom.
3. Arrange the classroom into a town hall set-up, with a table with chairs near the front, where the mayor and a few other citizens can sit, chairs for the plant personnel to the side facing the citizens, with the rest of the chairs in rows facing the front.

Activity Procedures

1. There is a flexible structure for the debate that follows a typical town hall meeting. The mayor will oversee the meeting and its progress.
2. The mayor calls the meeting to order and explains the purpose of the presentation. He or she also explains the proper procedures for making comments and asking questions. After the introduction, he or she turns the meeting over to the plant foreman who will oversee the plant personnel's presentation.
3. The plant foreman introduces his or her team, briefly discussing the job of each person. From this point, either the plant foreman or his or her designated speaker begins the presentation on the plant, how it works, and how it will benefit this community—remembering that this presentation should be persuasive in nature.
4. Citizens are given opportunities to ask questions of the plant personnel, make comments, and state their opinions.
5. Plant personnel will have the opportunity to make any final points, before the vote takes place.
6. Each citizen is given a ballot to vote for or against the placement of the plant in the community. To create suspense, the votes can be tallied by the teacher and shared with the class the following day.

Materials Needed

Ballots
Chairs and long table

Chapter 11

Atomic Structure, History, and the Periodic Table

Atomic Structure, History, and the Periodic Table Overview

The atom and its arrangement on the periodic table are the building blocks for matter. This unit is centered on the periodic table challenge project. This project is one that can extend through the years as students create their own periodic table square that becomes part of a large periodic table. Each year, students can challenge previous years' squares for the privilege of becoming part of the class periodic table. Be prepared for visitors for years to come as they return to see if their squares have "survived."

Depending on the grade level of the students, they may have received a lot of prior instruction on the periodic table, elements, and atoms. This unit takes students from their varied levels of prior knowledge and asks them to use the information in new ways. They will be asked to move beyond the basic memorization of elements and symbols into the relationships shown on the periodic table, the impact of atomic structure, and the history behind the discovery of our present knowledge of the atom.

Objectives for Atomic Structure, History, and the Periodic Table

By completing the lessons in this chapter, the students will be able to:
- describe the properties and locations of the subatomic particles in an atom;
- determine the numbers of subatomic particles in an atom, ion, or isotope;
- compare and show how the model of the atom has changed over time; and
- identify the groups and periods of the periodic table.

Chapter Activities

Below is an outline of the lessons included in this chapter. Depending on the prior knowledge of your students, you can pick which activities you want to use to reinforce the concepts. I suggest that you start with the project introduction so that all of the information and concepts presented during class will tie back into the project.

Lesson 50 introduces the period table challenge project in which students create a square for the large classroom periodic table. This lesson discusses how the periodic squares will be designed, as well as how they will be evaluated. In Lesson 51, students research the various scientists who have played a role in the determination of the atom's structure. After researching the various scientists, students will be given the challenge to create a timeline of the scientists and their contribution to the study of the atom.

Making a small, seemingly invisible substance interactive and interesting can be a challenge. Lesson 52 makes the atoms "come to life" as it asks the students to become subatomic particles as they create various atoms. The atoms become increasing more complex and students need to really understand atomic structure in order to create them.

After learning about atoms, Lesson 53 takes students to the next level, investigating ions and isotopes. Students are given element bags with various components in them. Using their knowledge of ions, isotopes and stable atoms, they will determine what elements their bags contain. After students complete their periodic table square on their own, Lesson 54 provides opportunity to share their efforts with their peers. In this activity, students make a defense to explain why their square represents their element well and should be placed on the class periodic table.

Vocabulary for This Chapter

atomic mass unit (AMU): the unit of mass for the periodic table, based on the atomic mass of carbon

atomic mass number: the average mass of an element, can be used to calculate the number of protons and electrons in an atom; shown on the periodic table

atomic number: the number of protons in an atom's nucleus

chemical symbol: a shorthand way to write the name of an element

electron: high-energy, low-mass subatomic particles that move around an atom's nucleus

electron cloud: region surrounding the nucleus of the atom where electrons most likely are found

group or family: in the periodic table, each of the 18 vertical columns of elements; each group (family) is made up of elements with similar properties

ion: a positively or negatively charged atom

isotopes: an atom of an element that has different numbers of neutrons; for example, Carbon-12 and Carbon-14

neutron: atomic particle with no charge (neutral) that is part of an atom's nucleus

nucleus: the positively charged center of atoms that contains protons and neutrons

oxidation number: a positive or negative number that indicates how many electrons an atom has lost, gained, or shared when bonding with other elements.

period: a horizontal row in the periodic table

proton: atomic particle with a positive charge that is part of atom's nucleus

valance electrons: the electrons in the outermost orbit of an atom that are involved in the bonding of the atom

Lesson 50

Subjects and Skills	Science, Language Arts, History
Rationale	This activity encourages students to create a well-thought-out product that can stand the test of time and analyze previously created products.
Objectives	Students will (1) develop a representational square of an element from the periodic table.
Activity Preparation	1. Develop a method for students to reserve the periodic table square that they will be challenging. If you have a large printed classroom periodic table, an effective way to handle this process is to have students record their names on sticky notes and attach them to their chosen squares on the classroom periodic table. If the square they want already has been taken, they will need to make another choice. 2. Decide where the periodic table will be displayed—the squares can be as small as bricks, or as large as ceiling tiles.
Activity Procedures	1. Give each student a copy of the Periodic Table Challenge Rubric (p. 176) and have him or her record his or her chosen element on the rubric. Students should also receive a copy of the Periodic Table Square Setup (p. 177). 2. The project is worth up to 160 points, rather than the usual 100 points, although the grade still can be recorded as a percentage. Discuss each criterion with the students, providing examples and explanations for excellent, good, fair, and poor.
Materials Needed	Paper for periodic table squares Periodic Table Challenge Project Rubric (p. 176) Periodic Table Square Setup (p. 177)

Name: _____ Date: _____

Periodic Table Challenge Project Rubric

Criteria	Excellent	Good	Fair	Poor
Standard Format	40 *points* Square is appropriate size; all information is in correct place.	30 *points* Square is not appropriate size; all information is in correct place.		0 *points* Square is not appropriate size; all information is not in correct place.
Atomic Number, Atomic Mass, Electron Configuration	10 *points* Atomic number, atomic mass, and electron configuration is correct and in the right format.		5 *points* One of the numbers/ information is incorrect or in the wrong format.	0 *points* Two or more of the numbers are missing or incorrect.
Symbol, Name Symbol and name are correct on the square.	10 *points* Symbol is the correct color and accurate with name.		5 *points* Symbol is not the correct color, but is accurate with name.	0 *points* Symbol or name is inaccurate.
State of Matter, Two Points Includes the element's state of matter and two of its points (boiling, freezing, melting).	10 *points* The element's state of matter is correct; includes two of its points.		5 *points* Includes the element's state of matter and one of its points.	0 *points* Missing states of matter or points.
Element Discovery and History	15 *points* Includes who discovered element; how, where, and when it was discovered; and interesting historical facts.	10 *points* Includes who discovered element and how, where, and when it was discovered.	5 *points* Includes who discovered element and where and when it was discovered.	0 *points* Information is missing or only includes who and when of discovery.
Everyday Uses Includes five everyday uses, or if not in use, why it is not commonly used.	15 *points* Includes five well-chosen everyday uses, or if element is not in use, why it is not commonly used.	10 *points* Includes less than five uses or uses are poorly chosen.		0 *points* No uses present.
Location on Earth	15 *points* Specific, explained information as to element's location on Earth.		5 *points* Unspecific information as to where element can be found on Earth.	0 *points* Location on Earth not present.
Creativity of Design Square is specific for the element, creative in its design.	20 *points* Square is specific for the element, creative in its design, shows large amount of work put into project.	12 *points* Design is creative, but not specific to the element.	8 *points* Basic design; not very specific or creative.	0 *points* No real time or effort put into design; not specific to element.
Use of Color Color is used on square; specific to element.	15 *points* Color used on square is specific and significant to element.	10 *points* Color is used on square; not specific to element.		0 *points* Does not have any color.
Placement in Periodic Table Incorrectly sized squares may not replace current squares.	10 *points* Square wins challenge, replaces current square in the class table.			0 *points* Square is not the correct size; has incorrect information.

Total Grade: _____
(Out of 160)

Periodic Table Square Setup

Atomic Number   **Valence Number**   **Mass Rounded to the Nearest Tenth**

At Least 5 Uses   **The Points**

S

Where It Can Be Found On Earth   **Element Name**   **History**

Electron Configuration
2, 8 . . . etc.

Lesson 51

ATOMIC GREATS

Subjects and Skills Science, Language Arts, History

Rationale This activity exposes students to the work of famous scientists.

Objectives Students will (1) create a timeline that is in chronological order and (2) detail the contributions of significant scientists in the area of the structure of the atom.

Activity Preparation
1. Decide whether this activity will be done in groups or individually and provide materials accordingly.
2. Determine the depth of research students will conduct. This usually is based on time. If there is more time for this activity, students can research the various "atomic" scientists using the Internet. If time is shorter, gather reference materials that classmates can share during a class period.

Activity Procedures
1. Students are given the following scientists to research: J. J. Thomson, Democritus, Ernest Rutherford, James Chadwick, John Dalton, and Niels Bohr.
2. They will need to research each scientist to find out what each discovered, how he helped in the progress of study of the atom, and any experimentation that took place as part of his discovery. Students also should note any other historic events taking place during the same years as the scientists' research.
3. Given a 1.5 meter length of adding machine tape, students will need to decide how to design their timelines on the tape. Well-constructed timelines will be colorful and complete with equal, labeled time divisions.
4. Scientists should be placed appropriately on the timeline with all of the information that has been gathered through research. A picture or drawing of the atom model associated with each scientist also should be included on the timeline.
5. At least 10 other significant historical, but not necessarily scientific, events should be added to the timeline, with an illustration for each.

Materials Needed Adding machine tape (1.5 meter lengths)
Film canisters (empty for transporting timelines)
Markers or colored pencils
Tape

Lesson 52

YOU BE THE ATOM!

Subjects and Skills	Science, Drama
Rationale	This activity uses a model to make an abstract concept more concrete.
Objectives	Students will be able to (1) identify characteristics of protons, neutrons, and electrons; (2) calculate the number of each subatomic particle; and (3) properly place electrons in their orbits.
Activity Preparation	1. This activity works best in a large area. 2. Prepare element cards by writing the symbol, atomic mass, and atomic number for the elements 1–10.
Activity Procedures	1. Ask students to describe the make-up of the lead in their pencil. Continue to question them until they have brainstormed that it is made up of atoms—carbon atoms to be specific. 2. Pose the questions: Are atoms the smallest piece of anything? What makes up atoms? 3. Students may have a lot of prior knowledge about atoms and subatomic particles. If not, this is the opportunity to introduce protons, neutrons, and electrons. 4. For groups with prior knowledge, ask them to describe each subatomic particle and its location. Although these particles are not living things, if the students do not have prior knowledge of this topic, it helps to discuss the characteristics of each subatomic particle through personification, with the protons being the positive energetic "beings" inside the nucleus with the dull beings that only take up space (neutrons), and the electrons represented as the negative, speedy beings running around the outside in their own little orbits. 5. Explain that students will get to have some fun creating human atoms. They can be creative in their personification of the subatomic particles. If they are protons, they may show this through being the "cheerleader" of the atom, while the electrons, running around the outside may not have the best attitudes. Luckily, there is a positive influence for every negative one in an electrically stable atom. 6. Begin with an atom with enough particles so that all students are involved. 7. Hold up an element card, explain that the atomic number determines the number of protons. Have students volunteer to be protons. They should get up and move to the center of the room. Although being positive may not be a quiet role, it needs to be quiet until all human particles are in place.

8. Explain that for every positive, there is a negative super small electron. Again, have students volunteer to be negative. If students need to understand the electron configurations, this is an opportunity to bring this into the discussion.

9. Lastly, explain that because the electron is so small, it does not have any impact on the mass of the atom. Therefore, the atomic mass must represent the protons and neutrons. Have students calculate the number of neutrons needed for the class atom. Again solicit volunteers to be neutrons.

10. Once everyone is in place, the atom can be set in motion, with the protons being overly positive, the electrons circling the outside in a negative way, and the neutrons simply standing in the nucleus taking up space.

11. Students may need additional large group practice in calculating the number of each particle and creating large atoms.

12. Once students feel secure in how to create atoms, break them into smaller groups for the human atom challenge.

13. Once students are separated, show one of the element cards for a "smaller" element. Each group now tries to be the first to create the correct representation of the element, using people as particles. This is very noisy, but the students laugh a lot and enjoy trying to be the first to figure out how to represent the atom.

14. Challenge the groups with different elements until the concepts are understood.

15. An extension would be to introduce isotopes and ions, and have students change their human atoms to an ion or an isotope.

....

Materials Needed   Index cards
Periodic table

Lesson 53

GOT MY EYE ON IONS!

Subjects and Skills	Science, Mathematics
Rationale	This activity teaches an abstract concept in a concrete manner.
Objectives	Students will be able to (1) distinguish isotopes and ions from stable atoms.

Activity Preparation

1. Create ion and isotope bags using the following list (lentils represent electrons, white beans represent neutrons, and pinto beans represent protons).
   - Bag 1: Carbon-14: 6 lentils, 8 white beans, 6 pinto beans.
   - Bag 2: Chlorine Ion: 18 lentils, 18 white beans, 17 pinto beans.
   - Bag 3: Oxygen Ion: 10 lentils, 8 white beans, 8 pinto beans.
   - Bag 4: Oxygen-18: 8 lentils, 10 white beans, 8 pinto beans.
   - Bag 5: Stable Oxygen: 8 lentils, 8 white beans, 8 pinto beans.
   - Bag 6: Magnesium Ion: 10 lentils, 12 white beans, 12 pinto beans.
   - Bag 7: Aluminum Ion: 10 lentils, 14 white beans, 13 pinto beans.
   - Bag 8: Hydrogen-3: 1 lentil, 2 white beans, 1 pinto bean.
   - Bag 9: Phosphorus-30: 15 lentils, 15 white beans, 15 pinto beans.
   - Bag 10: Lithium-6: 3 lentils, 3 white beans, 3 pinto beans.
   - Bag 11: Potassium Ion: 18 lentils, 20 white beans, 19 pinto beans.
   - Bag 12: Helium-3: 2 lentils, 1 white bean, 2 pinto beans.
   - Bag 13: Stable Lithium: 3 lentils, 4 white beans, 3 pinto beans.
   - Bag 14: Sulfur-33 Ion: 18 lentils, 17 white beans, 16 pinto beans.

Activity Procedures

1. Review how to use the periodic table to calculate electrically stable atoms. Reinforce that the atomic number or number of protons defines the element. If the number of protons is changed, it now is a new element.
2. Present the idea that not all atoms of an element "match" the periodic table. There can be different numbers of electrons (ions) or neutrons (isotopes).
3. Pose this problem: Given a substance in which the number of protons, neutrons, and electrons are known, how could it be determined if it is an electrically stable atom, an isotope, or an ion?
4. Allow students to share their various ideas. Put their ideas to the test by asking them to fill in the Isotope and Ion Data Table to identify the bags' contents.
5. Have students either share the bags among the groups or rotate to centers, in order to count, record, and process each bag's element.

Materials Needed (per group)

Lentils
White beans
Pinto beans
Zip-closing bags
Isotope and Ion Data Table (p. 182)

Atomic Structure, History, and the Periodic Table

Isotope and Ion Data Table

Bag Number	Number of Protons (brown)	Number of Neutrons (white)	Number of Electrons (smallest)	Ion, Isotope, or Electrically Stable Element?	Name of Bag's "Element"
1					
2					
3					
4					
5					
6					
7					
8					
9					
10					
11					
12					
13					
14					

Lesson 54

Subjects and Skills   Science, Oral Presentation Skills

Rationale   This activity provides an opportunity for students to analyze other students' work and present ideas about why their project is outstanding.

Objectives   Students will (1) critique a preexisting periodic table square project and (2) present the special qualities of their project.

Activity Preparation

1. Remind students about appropriate behavior during presentations and using valid, constructive criticism.

Activity Procedures

1. Students will need to make a simple recording chart for their votes. It should have three columns, one column for the symbol of the element and a yes and no column. As each student presents, the audience will record the symbol and after hearing the rationale, will vote on its placement in the permanent classroom periodic table. (Note: There are certain criteria that automatically will result in not being placed on the table, such as the square is not cut to the correct size, or if the student did not follow the correct format.)
2. Each student should stand next to or underneath the periodic table with the square they are challenging. They then will have 2–3 minutes to create their case for why their square is better than the preexisting one. If this is the first year, they will have to make a case for why their square meets the criteria in such a way as to deserve being placed on the classroom periodic table.
3. After each brief presentation, the audience will have a moment to record their votes. Once all presentations are complete, collect all the voting tables and tabulate the results.
4. Squares that are being replaced will be removed and replaced with the "winning" squares. The goal is that each year, the table gets better and better, and harder to defeat, so the level of research and creativity increases.

Materials Needed   Student periodic table squares

Chapter 12

Physical and Chemical Changes

Physical and Chemical Changes Overview

Physical and chemical changes happen on a daily basis. Children observe them but rarely question their occurrence. This unit asks students to analyze the different types of changes, discuss their intricacies, and become more aware of the occurrences in the world around them. Sometimes there is just not enough time for an in-depth science fair project, but students still enjoy developing and sharing their own experiments with others. The project in this unit has students choosing an experiment they would like to investigate and present to their classmates. The activities in the unit reinforce the ideas students will need in order to present their experiments to their peers.

Objectives for Physical and Chemical Changes

By completing the lessons in this chapter, the students will be able to:
- determine if a physical or chemical change has taken place,
- explain characteristics of physical and chemical changes, and
- identify properties of homogenous and heterogeneous mixtures.

Chapter Activities

Below is an outline of the lessons included in this chapter. Depending on the prior knowledge of your students, you can pick which activities you want to use to reinforce the concepts. I suggest that you start with the project introduction so that all of the information and concepts presented during the class will tie back into the project.

Lesson 55 introduces the project and its expectations. In this project, students will be given the opportunity to choose or design their own experiments, which they will present for their classmates. After an explanation of the project, students will begin looking for the experiment they would like to present to the class.

Lesson 56 is a very basic introduction to physical changes. Students will identify and conduct various physical changes to a piece of paper, all the while realizing that it stills remains a piece a paper even if it changes size, shape, or color.

Students will begin Lesson 57 by brainstorming various physical and chemical changes, as well as physical and chemical properties. They will then categorize all of the brainstormed ideas on a class bulletin board or large wall space. Lesson 58 exposes students to the two different classifications of mixtures. Students will bring food items from home to create edible mixtures and once created, they will analyze these edible heterogeneous and homogenous substances.

In Lesson 59, students will be using their imagination to create cartoon representations of the four basic types of chemical reactions: synthesis, decomposition, and single and double displacement. After students have chosen their experiments in Lesson 55 and spent some time developing them, Lesson 60 provides the guidelines and classroom management strategies for the final presentation of all of the experiments.

....

Vocabulary for This Chapter

chemical change: the change of substances to different substances

chemical formula: a precise statement that tells which elements are in a compound and their ratios

chemical property: a characteristic of a substance that indicates whether it can undergo a specific chemical change

combustibility: the ability of a substance to combust and burn easily

compound: substance made of the combined atoms of two or more elements

decomposition reactions: a chemical reaction in which a substance breaks down (decomposes) into two or more simpler substances

double displacement (replacement) reactions: chemical reaction in which two ionic compounds in a solution react, forming a precipitate, gas or water

endothermic reaction: a chemical reaction in which energy is absorbed

exothermic reaction: a chemical reaction is which energy is released

heterogeneous mixture: a mixture in which different parts can be easily distinguished

homogenous mixture: a mixture in which different materials are blended evenly so that the mixture is the same throughout; also called a solution

Law of Conservation of Mass: a law stating that matter is neither created nor destroyed during a chemical change

physical change: a change in size, shape, color, or state of matter

physical property: any characteristic of a material that can be observed without changing the identity of the material itself

product: in a chemical reaction, the substances produced by the reaction

reactant: the starting substances in a chemical reaction

single displacement (replacement) reactions: a chemical reaction in which one element replaces another element in a compound

synthesis reactions: a chemical reaction in which two or more substances combine to form a different substance

Lesson 55

Subjects and Skills	Science, Language Arts
Rationale	This activity allows students the freedom to choose and develop their own experiment.
Objectives	Students will be able to (1) explain the criteria for this project and (2) express their interest in performing an experiment of their choice.

Activity Preparation

1. Determine the materials, equipment, and resources students can utilize for their experiments. These will need to be shared before students decide the experiment they would like to conduct.
2. Decide if this project will be a partner or individual project; this decision is usually controlled by the amount of time available for presenting the experiments.

Activity Procedures

1. Introduce the project by asking students to brainstorm and share various demonstrations and experiments they have seen or wanted to conduct.
2. Once the list has been brainstormed, discuss the feasibility (materials, safety, etc.) of conducting and presenting each of the experiments in the classroom.
3. Give each student a copy of the Create Your Own Experiment Rubric (p. 188).
4. The project is worth up to 150 points, rather than the usual 100 points, although the grade still can be recorded as a percentage. Discuss each criterion with the students, providing examples and explanations for excellent, good, fair, and poor.
5. Encourage students to give examples of each step of the scientific method to clarify their knowledge.
6. Once students understand the depth necessary for conducting and presenting their experiment, they will need some time to choose their experiment. Students should avoid experiments that take a long time to conduct. All experiments should be able to be completed from start to finish in no more than 5–8 minutes. They should not select a "cooking show" type experiment where they mix something, put it in an "oven," and bring out a completed product a few seconds later.

Materials Needed

Experiment books for reference
Create Your Own Experiment Rubric (p. 188)
Various recycled materials students can use for their experiments

Name: _____ Date: _____

Create Your Own Experiment Rubric

Criteria	Excellent	Good	Fair	Poor
Title Experiment has an appropriate title.	5 *points* Title is appropriate, unique, and represents experiment.	3 *points* Title is appropriate and representative, but not unique.	1 *point* Title is present, but not significant to experiment.	0 *points* Title is not present.
Problem/Purpose Experiment problem stated as question; purpose stated as sentence.	5 *points* Problem and purpose both present, appropriate, and in correct format/punctuation.	3 *points* Problem and purpose both present and have correct punctuation but in wrong format.	1 *point* Problem and purpose present, but do not have the correct format or punctuation.	0 *points* Problem and purpose not present.
Hypothesis	15 *points* Relates to problem, defends reasoning for hypothesis.	12 *points* Relates to problem, has some reasoning for hypothesis selection.	8 *points* Somewhat related to problem, reasoning is weak.	0 *points* Not present or not related to the problem.
Materials All materials are listed and exact in description (i.e., includes measurements).	10 *points* All materials are listed and exact in description.	8 *points* Missing no more than 1 item on list, descriptions are exact.	6 *points* Missing no more than 2 items on list, 90% of descriptions are exact.	0 *points* Materials list is incomplete or more than 90% are inexact.
Procedure Procedures sequential, exact, allow for others to repeat experiment.	20 *points* Procedures sequential, easy to follow, exact, easy to read.	15 *points* Procedures sequential, easy to follow, could be more exact.	8 *points* Procedures are not sequential or somewhat hard to follow.	0 *points* Procedures are not present or very difficult to follow.
Data Data are appropriate, easy to read and understand; table has proper units, titles, and descriptions; graph and axis have proper units, titles, and descriptions.	30 *points* Data are recorded appropriately; easy to read and understand; table has proper units, titles, and descriptions; graph and axis have proper units, titles, and descriptions; data are represented clearly.	24 *points* Data are recorded appropriately; easy to read and understand; table has title, but has 1–2 numbers missing units and descriptions; graph and axis are titled, but has 1–2 numbers missing units and descriptions.	16 *points* Data table has no title or has more than three numbers without units and descriptions; graph and axis has no title or has more than three numbers without units and descriptions.	0 *points* No data present.
Conclusion	25 *points* Paragraph revisits hypothesis, explains how the lab was conducted, suggests a margin for error, and makes a new hypothesis if needed.	20 *points* Paragraph revisits hypothesis, explains how the lab was conducted, and makes a new hypothesis if needed. Does not suggest errors.	15 *points* Paragraph revisits hypothesis, explains how the lab was conducted.	0 *points* Conclusion not present or it does not revisit hypothesis.
Presentation Content Experiment follows scientific process, introduces materials, describes steps, and explains results.	20 *points* Experiment follows scientific process, introduces materials, describes steps, and clearly explains results; information is correct.	15 *points* Experiment follows scientific process, information is correct, introduces materials, and describes steps. Explanation unclear.	10 *points* Experiment incomplete or incorrect, describes steps and materials but has no explanation of results.	0 *points* Presentation does not follow intended experiment.
Presentation Flow	20 *points* Presenter understands topic, has practiced, and presentation flows well.	12 *points* Presentation has a few points of distraction, presenter understands topic.	8 *points* Presenter needs more practice or does not understand topic very well.	0 *points* Presentation not completed or given.

Total Grade: _____
(Out of 150)

Lesson 56

CUT IT, COLOR IT, OR CHANGE IT

Subjects and Skills   Science

Rationale   This activity introduces physical and chemical changes in a concrete and easily understood manner.

Objectives   Students will be able to (1) identify common examples of physical changes, (2) explain how to determine if a physical change has taken place, and (3) distinguish between physical and chemical changes.

Activity Procedures

1. Each student will need a blank piece of paper on his or her desk. Explain that this activity is an exercise in following directions.
2. Make a data table large enough for everyone to see, with the main category titled "physical properties." Title the other categories "size," "shape," and "state of matter."
3. Ask students to describe the paper in front of them. As ideas are shared, record them briefly in the appropriate category. Finish by asking what the object really is: a piece of paper.
4. Have students tear the paper in half.
5. Again ask them again to provide observations and record any different ideas. Finish by asking what the object is made of. (It is still paper.)
6. Tell students that they need to change their paper in a new way, as long as it is still paper after the change.
7. Have students share how they changed their paper. Derive that these ideas will need a new column, because they are not properties, but changes instead.
8. Continue through another four or five changes, allowing students to change the paper in their own way. Each time note how it impacted the properties of the paper. Remind students that although these changes have taken place, it is nonetheless still paper after the change.
9. Wrap up this activity by discussing what it means to have physical changes take place and how they are evidenced.
10. Students should be able to provide multiple examples of physical changes that happen to them on a daily basis.

Materials Needed   Scrap paper (letter size)

Lesson 57

THE WALL OF CHANGES

Subjects and Skills	Science, Language Arts
Rationale	This activity encourages students to use their creativity and apply chemistry concepts to the world around them.
Objectives	Students will be able to (1) identify common examples of physical and chemical changes, (2) explain how to determine if a physical or chemical change has taken place, and (3) distinguish between physical and chemical changes.
Activity Preparation	1. Prepare bulletin board or wall space for the placement of various brainstormed ideas by creating two areas, one labeled physical changes and one labeled chemical changes.
Activity Procedures	1. Review the paper-changing lesson on physical changes. Ask students to describe, define and explain the characteristics of a physical change.
	2. Introduce chemical changes, and how they are different than physical changes.
	3. Ask each group to create a Venn diagram comparing physical and chemical changes.
	4. Have each group share its perspectives on these two types of changes.
	5. Ask each group to brainstorm as many different physical and chemical changes as possible. Each change should be recorded on a sticky note.
	6. Students should be as creative as possible. Their goal is to list as many changes as possible that no other group brainstormed.
	7. Once groups have finished, they should place their sticky notes in the designated physical/chemical change area created in the classroom. If any two changes are the same, those two sticky notes are removed from the area.
	8. Groups should then be given a few moments to confirm that they agree with everyone's categorization of their sticky notes.
Materials Needed (per group)	Markers Sticky notes or pieces of paper

Lesson 58

MIXING MIXTURES LAB

Subjects and Skills Science, Language Arts

Rationale This activity allows students to create and analyze mixtures that could be found in the everyday world.

Objectives Students will be able to (1) identify characteristics of heterogeneous and homogenous mixtures and (2) distinguish between mixtures and compounds.

Activity Preparation
1. Divide the classroom into groups and assign food items for each group to supply by the end of the week. They will want to bring fresh items, not the stale ones in the back of the pantry. Taking into account the number of students divide the food as follows:
   - 50% bring cereal (approximately one cup each, whatever fresh cereal they have at home),
   - 30% bring various kinds of M&Ms (one 1.7 oz. bag; you may have to select a different snack food if peanut allergies are a concern in your school district), and
   - 20% bring pretzels (approximately one cup each, or a small snack size bag will work well).
2. The day before conducting the lab, remind students about providing food. Although this activity can be done without students providing food, it creates more variety in the mixture when they bring the components. Teachers may want to have extras of each type of food on hand for students who cannot afford to bring food or who forget to bring in their food for the day.
3. When making the powdered drink mix, make enough solution for each student to have a glass of solution with the mixture they will be preparing.

Activity Procedure
1. Have students contribute their food items to the large classroom mixture in the large bag or bucket. Stir or shake the mixture as each substance is added. This becomes Mixture 1.
2. Distribute the Mixing Mixture Lab handout (pp. 193–194) and a large sample of Mixture 1 for each group.
3. Distribute cups of the liquid solution, Mixture 2 (i.e., drink made from powder).
4. Allow students to make and record their observations. Although the intent is to eventually allow students to consume both mixtures, all observations should be made before any eating or drinking of the mixtures.

Physical and Chemical Changes

Materials Needed   Cups for drinks
Food provided by students
Large clean bag or plastic bucket
Napkins or paper towels
Powdered drink mix
Mixing Mixtures Lab handout (pp. 193–194)

Mixing Mixtures Lab

1. Define mixture.

   _____

   _____

2. Distinguish between a homogenous mixture and heterogeneous mixture.

   _____

   _____

3. How is a mixture different from a compound?

   _____

   _____

4. Name all of the ingredients in Mixture 1. Name all of the ingredients in Mixture 2.

   _____

   _____

   _____

5. Name 10 characteristics of Mixture 1. Name 10 characteristics of Mixture 2.

   _____

   _____

   _____

   _____

6. How are Mixtures 1 and 2 different? How are they alike?

   _____

   _____

   _____

7. What is a physical change? What is a chemical change?

   _____

   _____

   _____

8. When created, did the ingredients in Mixture 1 and Mixture 2 go through a physical or a chemical change? How do you know?

_____

_____

9. What type of mixture (homogenous or heterogeneous) is Mixture 1? Mixture 2?

_____

10. How could you separate each type of mixture?

_____

_____

11. Name three mixtures you see on a daily basis and tell whether they are homogenous or heterogeneous and how you would separate each one.

_____

_____

_____

_____

_____

12. Complete the table below.

Item	Mixture or Substance?	If It's a Mixture, How Could You Separate It?
Salt and pepper		
Sugar and iron		
Cake		
Nails and sawdust		
Soda		
Salad		
Tacos		
Cereal and milk		

Lesson 59

CREATIVE CHEMICAL CHANGE CARTOONS

Subjects and Skills Science, Language Arts, Art

Rationale Students will be using their imaginations and creativity to create cartoon representations of the four basic types of chemical reactions in order to make them easier to understand and remember.

Objectives Students will be able to (1) identify characteristics of the four basic types of chemical reactions: synthesis, decomposition, and single and double displacement; and (2) represent each type graphically.

Activity Preparation
1. Review the differences between physical and chemical changes.
2. Brainstorm all observations that may indicate a chemical change.

Activity Procedures
1. Introduce synthesis reactions by using an analogy of choice such as boy meets girl. No matter the situation, one element should "complete" the other.
2. Show examples of synthesis chemical equations and discuss how they are written, noting the multiple reactants and single product.
3. Discuss decomposition reactions in a similar way (boy breaks up with girl). The bonds between the two elements have broken, and they have split.
4. Show examples of decomposition equations and discuss how they are written, noting the single reactant and multiple products.
5. Displacement or replacement reactions, both single and double reactions, can be discussed together, then distinguished based on grouping.
6. Show examples of each type of replacement equation and discuss how each is written, noting the multiple reactants and multiple products, including how they "change partners."
7. Provide students with various chemical equations and ask students to identify the type of reactions noted in each. Once students have mastered identifying each type of reaction, provide them with one equation for each type of chemical reaction. They must create four different cartoons that show what is happening to the atoms and molecules in each reaction.
8. Although some students will want to be literal, they certainly can be creative in circumstances of the reaction, as well as the bodies of the atoms themselves.
9. The cartoons should be colorful, and the cartoon reaction obvious enough that it can be matched with the written equation.

Materials Needed Markers or colored pencils
White paper

Lesson 60

Subjects and Skills   Science, Language Arts, Oral Presentation Skills

Rationale   This activity encourages students to use their scientific knowledge and vocabulary while sharing an experiment of personal interest.

Objectives   Students will be able to (1) share their chosen experiment with their peers, (2) discuss procedures as they are completed, and (3) explain how or why their experiment functions as it does.

Activity Preparation
1. Gather all materials that will need to be provided for students' experiments.
2. Decide on the order of the experimental presentations.
3. Lab reports will be submitted before the presentation so the presentation can be assessed for correctness.

Activity Procedures
1. Distribute safety goggles to audience.
2. Each student or pair will go to the designated area for their presentation.
3. They will begin by sharing the title, purpose or problem, and hypothesis for their experiment.
4. They should show each material necessary for their experiment by holding it up and saying its name.
5. Students then can begin conducting their experiment by explaining each step of the process. They should incorporate as much scientific vocabulary as possible.
6. If a chemical change has taken place, students should explain the reactants and products, as well as, if possible, the chemical equation that shows the chemical reaction. This presentation can be as in-depth as the students' level of knowledge allows.
7. After each presentation, the audience should be encouraged to ask questions.

Materials Needed   Materials specific to student experiments
Safety goggles for audience

Chapter 13

Acids, Bases, and Solutions

Acids, Bases, and Solutions Overview

Acids and bases surround us, from cleaning products, to the popular soft drinks that students enjoy drinking so much. Students may have prior knowledge about the existence of acids and bases, but do they know how they are used in the world around them? This unit introduces students to the various unique properties of both acids and bases, centering on a project that asks students to create a PowerPoint advertisement for a predetermined acid or base. Even if their acid or base is dangerous, after researching its uses, they have to create a positive outlook for its use. This challenges students to alter their negative perceptions of acids and bases.

Objectives for Acids, Bases, and Solutions

By completing the lessons in this chapter, the students will be able to:
- identify characteristics of common acids and bases,
- give examples of common acids and bases, and
- create and use an indicator to determine a substance's pH.

Chapter Activities

Lesson 61 introduces various real-world applications for acids and bases. It introduces the acid/base advertisement project in which students create a PowerPoint commercial for their chosen acid or base. Even though student may think strong acids and bases are dangerous, this activity asks students to looks at them from a new perspective by trying to "sell" their acid or base to an audience.

Lesson 62 reinforces the basic properties of acids and bases. After a little classroom discussion, it has students discussing and communicating the unique qualities of acids and bases, as well as their similarities. Lesson 63 has the science classroom smelling like cabbage as students create their own fresh indicator. Students then will use their homemade indicator to test various household substances in order to determine their pH, and identify them as acids or bases..

A local factory has asked for permission to dump their acidic and basic waste into the local water system. They will dilute it to 1 ppm. Is it safe to do so? Lesson 64 has students addressing this issue.

acid: a substance that produces hydrogen ions (H^+) in solution; acid solutions have a pH
of less than 7

base: a substance that produces hydroxide ions (OH^-) in solution; basic solutions have a
pH of more than 7

indicator: an organic compound that changes color in an acidic or basic solution

neutral: a substance with a pH of 7

potential of hydrogen (pH): a measure if hydronium ion (H_3O^+) concentration in solution;
expressed on the pH scale from 0 to 14. From 7 down to 0, a solution is increasingly
acidic; at 7 it is neutral (pure water) from 7 to 14, a solution is increasingly basic

Hands-On Physical Science

Lesson 61

Subjects and Skills	Science, Language Arts, Technology
Rationale	This activity asks students to use their creativity to look at acids and bases in a positive light.
Objectives	Students will develop and present to the class a PowerPoint commercial that (1) states the advantages and disadvantages of their substance and (2) makes a case for its purchase.

Activity Preparation

1. Make arrangements for access to computers, usually for 1–2 days during the unit.
2. Based on your school's technology appropriate-use policies, choose Web sites that the students can use to research their substances. If your classroom doesn't have access to the Web, you can print the information off some of these sites ahead of time.
3. Choose the acids and bases that students will research.
4. Place the names of the substances on slips of paper or cards. (Note: A brief list of common acids and bases has been included on p. 201.)

Activity Procedures

1. As each student enters the classroom, have him or her choose one of the acid or base cards.
2. Give each student a rubric for the commercial project and have him or her record his or her substance on the rubric.
3. The project is worth 100 points. Discuss each criterion with the students, providing examples and explanations for excellent, good, fair, and poor. Encourage students to give examples of each to clarify their knowledge.

Materials Needed

Acid and Base Advertisement Project Rubric (p. 200)
Common Acids and Bases (p. 201)
PowerPoint software

Name: _____ Date: _____

Acid and Base Advertisement Project Rubric

Criteria	Excellent	Good	Fair	Poor
Slogan	**15 *points*** A specific, memorable, creative slogan has been chosen for the substance.	**12 *points*** A specific slogan has been chosen for the substance; not very creative or memorable.	**8 *points*** A memorable, creative slogan has been chosen for the substance; not specific to the substance.	**0 *points*** Slogan is not present.
Description Substance is described, including both physical and chemical properties.	**15 *points*** Substance is described with multiple details, including both physical and chemical properties; uses scientific vocabulary.	**12 *points*** Substance is described with 3–4 details, including both physical and chemical properties; uses scientific vocabulary.	**8 *points*** Substance is described with 1–2 details; does not include properties.	**0 *points*** Substance is not described.
Location Found or Created If substance is found naturally, maps and information on its locations are included. If it is produced, descriptions and directions on its production are included.	**15 *points*** Specific maps and information on its locations are included, or if it is produced, specific descriptions and directions on its production are included.	**12 *points*** Does not include all of the details and information of where the substance was found or where and how it was created.	**8 *points*** Missing significant information about where the substance was found or where and how it was created.	**0 *points*** Information not present.
Useful or Harmful Explains whether the substance is useful or harmful. If it is harmful, warnings are included.	**10 *points*** Explains whether the substance is useful or harmful. Specific and complete warnings are included.	**7 *points*** Explains whether the substance is useful or harmful. If it is harmful, brief warnings are included.		**0 *points*** Explanation of use or harm is not present.
Uses Researches and shares multiple uses that impact our daily lives. Uses graphics and text to display impact.	**20 *points*** Researches and shares more than four uses that impact our daily lives. Includes at least one graphic to display impact.	**15 *points*** Researches and shares two to three uses that impact our daily lives.	**10 *points*** Shares at least three uses for the substance, but they are not related to everyday life.	**0 *points*** Uses are not included.
Pictures or Graphics	**15 *points*** At least three pictures and graphics have been chosen and included for their significance to the substance.	**10 *points*** One to two pictures and graphics have been chosen and included for their significance to the substance.	**5 *points*** Pictures and graphics have been chosen, but they are not significant to the substance.	**0 *points*** Pictures and graphics are not present.
Creativity of Slideshow	**10 *points*** Slideshow is distinctive to substance, including colors and animation.	**7 *points*** Slideshow is distinctive to substance, including colors or animation.		**0 *points*** Slideshow is not distinctive to substance.

Total Grade: _____
(Out of 100)

Common Acids and Bases

✳ Acetic Acid	✳ Ammonia	✳ Ascorbic Acid
✳ Calcium Hydroxide	✳ Carbonic Acid	✳ Chromic Acid
✳ Citric Acid	✳ Formic Acid	✳ Hydrochloric Acid
✳ Magnesium Hydroxide	✳ Nitric Acid	✳ Phosphoric Acid
✳ Potassium Hydroxide	✳ Prussic Acid	✳ Salicylic Acid
✳ Sodium Hydroxide	✳ Sulfuric Acid	✳ Tannic Acid
✳ Tartaric Acid	✳ Uric Acid	

Lesson 62

ACIDS, BASES, AND NEUTRALS? OH MY!

Subjects and Skills	Science, Language Arts
Rationale	This activity allows students to see a visual representation of the relationship between acids and bases.
Objectives	Students will (1) make simple observations to (2) develop a Venn diagram that compares and contrasts properties of acids and bases.
Activity Preparation	1. Duplicate and cut out the Acid and Base Categorization Cards (p. 203). Copy each set on different colored paper so there is one set for each group or pair of students.
Activity Procedures	1. Distribute the Acid and Base card sets to each pair or group of students.
	2. Using the card sets and either class sets of Venn diagram outlines or student-created outlines, have each group place the cards appropriately as they discuss the properties of acids, bases, and neutrals.
	3. After each group has decided on the proper placement, go through each item and discuss where various groups placed it.
	4. Each group should be able to defend their placement of the different properties.
	5. Once discussed, students can record their information in their own Venn diagrams.
Materials Needed	Acid and Base Categorization Cards (p. 203)

Acid and Base Categorization Cards

contributes H⁺ ions	contributes OH⁻ ions	soap
example: HCl	example: NaOH	salt
1–6 on the pH scale	8–14 on pH scale	ammonia
turns litmus paper red	turns litmus paper blue	electrolyte
tastes sour	tastes bitter	indicator
electrolyte	nonelectrolyte	no effect on indicator
does not change litmus paper	lemons	has neither H⁺ ions nor OH⁻ ions
7 on pH scale	water	has both H⁺ ions and OH⁻ ions

Lesson 63

Subjects and Skills	Science, Language Arts
Rationale	This activity exposes the students to real-world acids, bases, and indicators.
Objectives	Students will (1) create their own indicator and (2) use it to test various household substances in order to determine their pH.

Activity Preparation

1. Prepare all materials by placing them in labeled cups with eyedroppers or labeled dropper bottles.
2. Tear red cabbage into small pieces and store in a plastic bag. Note: Although the indicator can be prepared ahead of time and shared with students, this experience is much more meaningful if each group creates and tests the substances with its own fresh indicator. This reinforces the idea that this is a real-world substance that they could make at home.
3. Immediately before students enter the classroom, place the cabbage in the beakers. Fill each beaker approximately half full of loosely packed cabbage.

Activity Procedures

1. Immediately upon entering the classroom, students will need to begin preparing their indicator by obtaining a beaker with cabbage.
2. They should add enough water to the beaker to cover the cabbage.
3. The beakers with the cabbage can be placed on medium heat on the hot plates while the students begin working on their lab report.
4. Students should begin setting up their lab report with their purpose, followed by their predicted classification of each substance that they are going to test.
5. Next, they will predict the pH of each substance to be tested.
6. The indicator should now be ready. The water will be a deep purple color, and the cabbage will have turned white. Students should check with the teacher before using the indicator, to be sure it really is ready. It is safe to use hot; it will not change the results of the test.
7. After testing each substance with a few drops of indicator, students will use the indicator chart on their worksheets to decide what the pH was for each substance.
8. On their data table, they will use colored pencils to recreate the color that was produced when the indicator was added. Then, they will record the actual pH and whether the substance was an acid, base, or neutral.

Materials Needed
Ammonia
Antacid
Aspirin (ground and dissolved in distilled water)
250 ml beaker
Chem-trays or small-welled trays
Clear soda (Sprite, 7-Up)
Colored pencils
Detergent
Distilled water
Drain cleaner
Eyedroppers
Hot plate for each group
Hydrochloric acid
Lemon juice
Red cabbage
Tap water
What's That Smell? handout (p. 206)

What's That Smell?

pH	0	1	2	3	4	5	6	7	8	9	10	11	12	13	14
	ACIDIC ──────────────────────────────────► BASIC														
color	red		rose			purple		blue				green		yellow	

Red Cabbage pH Indicator Color Key

PROCEDURE

1. Before gathering any materials, look through your data table and record all of the substances you will using for this experiment, then record whether you think each substance is an acid, base, or neutral.
2. Next, record a predicted pH for each substance based on your predictions from Step 1. The pH you predict will be based on how strong you feel the acid or base may be.
3. Gather all the materials you need to complete your lab.
4. Carefully test each substance by adding 3–5 drops of indicator.
5. Using the above guide, decide what you think the pH was for each. On your data table, use colored pencils to recreate the color that was produced when the indicator was added. Then, record the actual pH and whether your substance was an acid, base, or neutral.
6. Clean all of your lab materials, including disposing of your cabbage by placing it in the garbage.

DATA TABLE

Substance	Predicted Acid, Base, or Neutral	Predicted pH	Actual Color	Actual pH	Acid, Base, or Neutral

QUESTIONS

1. In which of the substances tested would you expect to find the most free OH- ions? Which one would have the most free H+ ions? Why do you think this?

_____

_____

_____

_____

2. When tea and lemon juice are mixed, the color of the mixture lightens. Which of the two substances is acting as the indicator, and which is the acid or base? How do you know?

_____

_____

_____

_____

3. Why would I use a clear soda, like Sprite, and not a cola in this lab?

_____

_____

_____

_____

4. Record your conclusions about this lab on the lines below.

_____

_____

_____

_____

Lesson 64

CAN DILUTION BE THE SOLUTION?

Subjects and Skills   Science, Mathematics

Rationale   This activity addresses a real-world issue surrounding the disposal of industrial acids and bases.

Objectives   Students will (1) discuss and hypothesize the effectiveness of dilution for disposal of acids and bases and (2) conduct an investigation to confirm their hypothesis.

Activity Preparation
1. Review the characteristics and safety concerns of strong bases and acids.
2. Prepare dropper bottles of Mystery Substance 1 (HCl) and Mystery Substance 2 (NaOH).

Activity Procedures
1. Present the following situation to students: As is common practice with many factories, a local company uses strong acids and bases in its cleaning processes. It has asked for permission to dispose of these substances in the local water system. They will dilute the substances to 1 ppm (parts per million) before releasing it into the water. Is this a safe option? Should their proposal be accepted?
2. Have students brainstorm and share various questions and concerns that they would need answered to make an informed decision regarding this situation.
3. Discuss the process of dilution and how it takes place. Discuss what value is considered a safe pH for the flora and fauna in a water system.
4. Based on this information, students will make a hypothesis about the effectiveness of dilution and whether it will be safe for the company to use this method of disposal.
5. Distribute a random substance sample to each group by placing the sample in the first well of their welled tray.
6. Have them begin the dilution process by taking one drop from the "pure" substance and placing it in the next well.
7. Then add 9 drops of water to the well. This will be one part per 10 parts. (Note: If you are using a liquid indicator, students should only add 8 drops of water, and one drop of indicator, so it is 1 part per 10)
8. Remove one drop from the new well and put it in the next empty well. Again add 9 drops of water. This is now one part per 100 parts. (Note: Again, consider the use of liquid indicator and adjust the drops of water accordingly.)
9. Students will continue until they have a ratio of 1 part per million.

10. Once they have created all of the wells, students should test each well using litmus paper or indicator to determine the presence of the strong acid or base. If using an indicator, it works best if the tray is placed on a piece of white paper so the slight color variations can be seen easily.

11. Using this data, students will share their results and make conclusions on the safety of dilution.

Materials Needed (per group)	Beaker or glass
	Chem-trays or small welled trays
	Dropper bottle or eyedropper and cup
	HCl (muriatic acid)
	Litmus paper or indicator (can use leftover cabbage indicator from indicator lab)
	NaOH (drain cleaner)
	White paper

Can Dilution Be the Solution?

PROBLEM

As is common practice with many factories, a local company uses strong acids and bases in its cleaning processes. It has asked for permission to dispose of these substances in the local water system. It will dilute the substances to 1 ppm (parts per million) before releasing it into the water. Is this a safe option? Should their proposal be accepted?

HYPOTHESIS AND EXPLANATION OF DECISION

_____

_____

_____

_____

PROCEDURE

1. If your tray is not numbered, number your wells 1–8, or you are not using a tray, number your cups 1–8.
2. Place your mystery substance in the first well of your tray (Well 1).
3. Place 10 drops of water in Well 8. This will represent your neutral for comparison.
4. Using an eyedropper, place one drop of the "pure" substance from Well 1 in the next well (Well 2).
5. Add nine drops of water to Well 2. This will be one part (substance) per 10 parts (of solution).
6. Remove one drop from Well 2 and put it into Well 3. Again, add nine drops of water. This is now one part per 100 parts.
7. Remove one drop from Well 3 and put it into Well 4. Again, add nine drops of water. This is now one part per 1,000 parts.
8. Continue moving one drop from each well into the next, adding nine drops of water until you have a solution that represents one part per million parts.
9. Using your indicator, test the pH of each well.
10. Record your results in your data table.
11. Dispose of your materials.
12. Using your results, determine if dilution is a safe solution for disposing of the strong acids and bases.

DATA TABLE

Well Number	Color of Indicator	pH	Concentration
1			1
2			1/10
3			1/100
4			1/1000
5			1/10,000
6			1/100,000
7			1/1,000,000
8			Water (neutral)

QUESTIONS

1. Did you start with an acid or base? Do you think the effectiveness of dilution will be different for acids and bases?

_____

_____

_____

_____

2. Did your cups ever match Well 8, the neutral cup? If so, at what concentration did your wells become neutral? If not, do you think it would ever become neutral? Explain.

_____

_____

_____

_____

3. Compare your results with another group that tested another substance. How do your results compare to theirs?

_____

_____

_____

_____

4. Does your data support or refute the idea that dilution is a safe solution for disposal of strong acids and bases?

_____

_____

_____

_____

YOUR FINAL DECISION

Explain your final decision about the safety of dilution. Use your data in your explanation.

_____

_____

_____

_____

_____

_____

_____

_____

_____

_____

_____

Resources

Force and Motion/ Newton's Law's	O'Donnell, K. (2007). *Sir Isaac Newton: Using the laws of motion to solve problems.* New York: PowerKids Press. Schrier, E. (1987). *Newton at the bat: The science in sports.* New York: Scribner's. Speyer, E. (1994). *Six roads from Newton: Great discoveries in physics.* New York: Wiley.
Energy and Heat	Gunkel, D. (2006). *Alternative energy sources.* Detroit, MI: Greenhaven Press. Morris, N. (2007). *Geothermal power.* North Mankato, MN: Smart Apple Media. Oxlade, C. (2005). *Energy: Present knowledge, future trends.* North Mankato, MN: Smart Apple Media. Sherman, J. (2004). *Nuclear power.* Mankato, MN: Capstone Press.
Famous Scientist Product Resources	Anderson, M. (1999). *Scientists of the ancient world.* Springfield, NJ: Enslow Publishers. Bragg, M. (1998). *On giants' shoulders: Great scientists and their discoveries: From Archimedes to DNA.* New York: Wiley. Simmons, J. (1996). *The scientific 100: A ranking of the most influential scientists, past and present.* Secaucus, NJ: Carol Publishing.
States of Matter/Fluid Laws Unit	Bayrock, F. (2006). *States of matter: A question and answer book.* Mankato, MN: Capstone Press. Macrone, M. (1994). *Eureka!: What Archimedes really meant and 80 other key ideas explained.* New York: HarperCollins Publishers. Tabak, J. (2004). *Mathematics and the laws of nature: Developing the language of science.* New York: Facts On File.
Simple Machines	Glover, D. (1997). *Ramps and wedges.* Crystal Lake, IL: Rigby Interactive Library. Lampton, C. (1991). *Bathtubs, slides, roller coaster rails: Simple machines that are really inclined planes.* Brookfield, CT: Millbrook Press. Lampton, C. (1991). *Marbles, roller skates, doorknobs: Simple machines that are really wheels.* Brookfield, CT: Millbrook Press. Lampton, C. (1991). *Seesaws, nutcrackers, brooms: Simple machines that are really levers.* Brookfield, CT: Millbrook Press.
Mousetrap Car Resources	Balmer, A. (1997). *Mouse-trap cars: The secrets to success.* Austin, TX: Doc Fizzix Comix.

Kassinger, R. (2002). *Build a better mousetrap: Make classic inventions, discover your problem-solving genius, and take the inventor's challenge.* Hoboken, NJ: J. Wiley & Sons.

Renner, A. (1977). *How to build a better mousetrap car—and other experimental science fun.* New York: Dodd, Mead.

Electricity/Energy Conservation	Gardner, R. (1992). *Experimenting with energy conservation.* New York: Franklin Watts.
	Hunter, R. (2005). *The facts about electricity.* North Mankato, MN: Smart Apple Media.
	Tomecek, S. (2003). *What a great idea!: Inventions that changed the world.* New York: Scholastic Nonfiction.

Magnetism	Flaherty, M. (1999). *Magnetism & magnets.* Brookfield, CT: Copper Beech Books.
	Gardner, R. (1994). *Electricity and magnetism.* New York: Twenty-First Century Books.
	Hirschmann, K. (2006). *Magnets.* Farmington Hills, MI: KidHaven Press.
	Kerrod, R. (2002). *The way science works.* London: DK.

Waves/Sound and Light	Isaacs, A. (2005). *Characteristics and behaviors of waves: Understanding sound and electromagnetic waves.* New York: Rosen.
	Karpelenia, J. (2004). *Light.* Logan, IA: Perfection Learning.
	Parker, S. (2005). *Making waves: Sound.* Chicago: Heinemann Library.
	Stille, D. (2006). *Manipulating light: Reflection, refraction, and absorption.* Minneapolis, MN: Compass Point Books.

Musical Instrument Project	Fiarotta, N. (1993). *Music crafts for kids: The how-to book of music discovery.* New York: Sterling.
	Hopkin, B. (1995). *Making simple musical instruments.* Asheville, NC: Lark Books.
	McLean, M. (1988). *Make your own musical instruments.* Minneapolis, MN: Lerner.

Nuclear Energy/Town Hall Debate	Ball, J. (2003). *Nuclear energy.* Milwaukee, WI: Gareth Stevens Publishers.
	Giacobello, J. (2003). *Nuclear power of the future: New ways of turning atoms into energy.* New York: Rosen.
	Graham, I. (1999). *Nuclear power.* Austin, TX: Raintree, Steck-Vaughn Publishers.
	Kidd, J. (1999). *Quarks and sparks: The story of nuclear power.* New York: Facts On File.

Atomic Structure/ History and the Periodic Table	Ardley, N. (1989). *The world of the atom.* New York: Gloucester.
	Gallant, R. (1999). *The ever-changing atom.* New York: Benchmark Books.
	Goldstein, N. (2001). *How do we know the nature of the atom.* New York: Rosen.
	Pasachoff, N. (2003). *Niels Bohr: Physicist and humanitarian.* Berkeley Heights, NJ: Enslow Publishers.

Element Square Challenge	Miller, R. (2006). *The elements.* Minneapolis, MN: Twenty-First Century Books.
	Newton, D. (1999). *Chemical elements: From carbon to krypton* (Volume 1, A–F). Detroit, MI: UXL/Gale.
	Newton, D. (1999). *Chemical elements: from carbon to krypton* (Volume 2, G–O). Detroit, MI: UXL/Gale.
	Newton, D. (1999). *Chemical elements: from carbon to krypton* (Volume 3, P–Z). Detroit, MI: UXL/Gale.
	Stwertka, A. (2002). *A guide to the elements.* New York: Oxford University Press.

Student Created Experiment	Green, J. (2004). *Potato radio, dizzy dice, and more wacky, weird, experiments from the mad scientist.* New York: Perigee.
	Potter, J. (1995). *Science in seconds for kids: Over 100 experiments you can do in ten minutes or less.* New York: Jossey-Bass.
	Rybolt, T. (2004). *Soda pop science projects: Experiments with carbonated soft drinks.* Berkeley Heights, NJ: Enslow Publishers.
	VanCleave, J. (1999). *Janice VanCleave's 203 icy, freezing, frosty, cool & wild experiments.* New York: J. Wiley.

Acids and Bases	Firm, G. (1997). *Acids, bases and salts.* New York: Grolier Educational.
	Oxlade, C. (2002). *Acids and bases.* Chicago: Heinemann Library.
	Patten, J. (1995). *Acids and bases.* Vero Beach, FL: Rourke.

About the Author

Laurie Westphal learned science in the same manner as many other students, through the use of chapter questions, copying notes, and reading various chapters in the science textbook. After questioning this practice, she decided to teach science and to try and break out of the mold. Westphal was given the freedom to develop engaging product-based lessons and activities for her students, the kind of teaching she missed while in school. After using this method of teaching science for 14 years, both overseas and in the United States, as well as presenting staff development and working with gifted education, she now works as an independent gifted education and science consultant. Laurie has made it her goal to share her vision for real-world, product-based lessons that help students become scientific critical thinkers and effective problem solvers, rather than simply question answerers.